Welcome to
LIFESEARCH

If you urgently need to prepare to lead a LifeSearch group, turn the page and read QuickLead. QuickLead will give you enough information to get started.

L IFESEARCH hopes to help you and other persons within a small group explore topics about which you are concerned in your everyday living. We've tried to make LifeSearch

✔ immediately helpful to you;

✔ filled with practical ideas;

✔ Christian-oriented and biblically based;

✔ group building, so you will find companions in your mutual struggles and learning;

✔ easy for anyone to lead.

You have probably chosen to join with others in studying this LIFE-SEARCH book because you feel some need. You may feel that need in your life strongly. Our hope for you is that by the time you complete the six chapters in this book with your LifeSearch group, you will have

✔ a better handle on how to meet the need you feel;

✔ some greater insights into yourself;

✔ a deeper understanding of how Christian faith can help you meet that need;

✔ a more profound relationship with God;

✔ new and/or richer relationships with the other persons in your LifeSearch group.

If you discover nothing else as part of this LifeSearch experience, we want you to learn this fact: *that you are not alone as you face life.* Other people have faced and still face the same problems, struggles, demands, and needs that you face. Some have advice to offer. Some have learned things the hard way—things they can now tell you about. Some can help you think through and talk through old concerns and new insights. Some can listen as you share what you've tried and what you want to achieve. Some even need what you can offer.

And you will never be alone because God stands with you.

The secret to LifeSearch is in the workings of your group. No two LifeSearch groups will ever be alike. Your LifeSearch group is made up of unique individuals—including you. All of you have much to offer one another. This LifeSearch book simply provides a framework for you and your group to work together in learning about an area of mutual concern.

We would like to hear what you think about LifeSearch and ways you can suggest for improving future LifeSearch books. A Mail-In Feedback survey appears in the back. Whether you lead the group or participate in it, please take the time to fill out the survey and mail it in to us.

IF YOU ARE LEADING A LifeSearch GROUP, please read the articles in the back of this book. These LifeSearch group leadership articles may answer the questions you have about leading your group.

IF YOU ARE PARTICIPATING IN A LifeSearch GROUP, BUT NOT LEADING IT, please read at least the article, "If You're Not Leading the Group." In any case, **you will benefit most if you come to your group meeting having read the chapter ahead of time and having attempted any assignments given in the previous chapter's "Before Next Time" sections.**

We want to remain helpful to you throughout your LifeSearch group experience. If you have any questions about using this LifeSearch book, please feel free to call Curric-U-Phone at 1-800-251-8591, and ask for the LifeSearch editor.

QUICKLEAD™

Look here for **QUICK** information about how to **LEAD** a session of LIFE-SEARCH. On LIFESEARCH pages, look for the following:

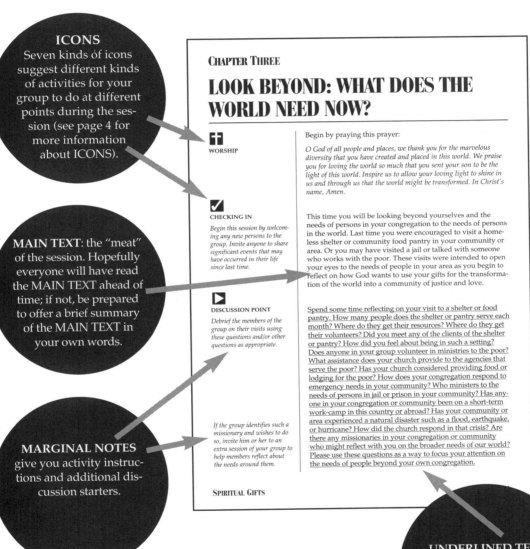

ICONS
Seven kinds of icons suggest different kinds of activities for your group to do at different points during the session (see page 4 for more information about ICONS).

MAIN TEXT: the "meat" of the session. Hopefully everyone will have read the MAIN TEXT ahead of time; if not, be prepared to offer a brief summary of the MAIN TEXT in your own words.

MARGINAL NOTES give you activity instructions and additional discussion starters.

CHAPTER THREE

LOOK BEYOND: WHAT DOES THE WORLD NEED NOW?

WORSHIP

Begin by praying this prayer:

O God of all people and places, we thank you for the marvelous diversity that you have created and placed in this world. We praise you for loving the world so much that you sent your son to be the light of this world. Inspire us to allow your loving light to shine in us and through us that the world might be transformed. In Christ's name, Amen.

CHECKING IN

Begin this session by welcoming any new persons to the group. Invite anyone to share significant events that may have occurred in their life since last time.

This time you will be looking beyond yourselves and the needs of persons in your congregation to the needs of persons in the world. Last time you were encouraged to visit a homeless shelter or community food pantry in your community or area. Or you may have visited a jail or talked with someone who works with the poor. These visits were intended to open your eyes to the needs of people in your area as you begin to reflect on how God wants to use your gifts for the transformation of the world into a community of justice and love.

DISCUSSION POINT

Debrief the members of the group on their visits using these questions and/or other questions as appropriate.

Spend some time reflecting on your visit to a shelter or food pantry. How many people does the shelter or pantry serve each month? Where do they get their resources? Where do they get their volunteers? Did you meet any of the clients of the shelter or pantry? How did you feel about being in such a setting? Does anyone in your group volunteer in ministries to the poor? What assistance does your church provide to the agencies that serve the poor? Has your church considered providing food or lodging for the poor? How does your congregation respond to emergency needs in your community? Who ministers to the needs of persons in jail or prison in your community? Has anyone in your congregation or community been on a short-term work-camp in this country or abroad? Has your community or area experienced a natural disaster such as a flood, earthquake, or hurricane? How did the church respond in that crisis? Are there any missionaries in your congregation or community who might reflect with you on the broader needs of our world? Please use these questions as a way to focus your attention on the needs of people beyond your own congregation.

If the group identifies such a missionary and wishes to do so, invite him or her to an extra session of your group to help members reflect about the needs around them.

SPIRITUAL GIFTS

UNDERLINED TEXT identify discussion starters inside the MAIN TEXT.

For more information, read the **LEADERSHIP ARTICLES** in the back of this LIFESEARCH book.

ICONS

ICONS are picture/symbols that show you at a glance what you should do with different parts of the main text at different times in the LIFESEARCH sessions.

The seven kinds of icons are

 WORSHIP—A prayer, hymn, or other act of worship is suggested at this place in the MAIN TEXT.

 CHECKING IN—At the beginning of each session, LIFESEARCH group members will be asked to "check in" with each other about what is happening in their lives. Sometimes group members will also be asked to "check in" about how their LIFESEARCH group experience seems to them.

 DISCUSSION POINT—Either the MAIN TEXT or a MARGINAL NOTE will suggest discussion starters. You will probably find more DISCUSSION POINTS than you can use in the usual LIFESEARCH session.

 GROUP INTERACTION—Either the MAIN TEXT or a MARGINAL NOTE will suggest a group activity that goes beyond a simple discussion within the whole group.

 BIBLE STUDY—At least once each session, your LIFESEARCH group will study a Bible passage together. Usually, DISCUSSION POINTS and/or GROUP INTERACTIONS are part of the BIBLE STUDY.

 WRITTEN REFLECTION—The MAIN TEXT will contain one or more suggestions for individuals to reflect personally on an issue. Space will be provided within the MAIN TEXT for writing down reflections. Sometimes individuals will be invited to share their written reflections if they wish.

 BEFORE NEXT TIME—In most sessions, your LIFESEARCH group members will be asked to do something on their own before the next time you meet together.

INTRODUCTION

This volume of LIFESEARCH will help you develop stronger parenting skills as a Christian.

The specific topics explored in this volume of LIFESEARCH speak to parents today. For example, self-image and self-esteem (chapter 1) are lifelong concerns. Parents of crawling babies, elementary students, and college students wonder what to do about discipline (chapter 2). No parent leads a stress-free life. Some cope well with stress, but all of us can use ideas for enhancing our coping skills (chapter 3). How to resolve conflicts (chapter 4) in ways that are just and caring demand skills that become increasingly important in a conflicted world. Faith is not something we can assume children will have, and nurturing a child's faith needs to be added to a Christian's list of intentional goals (chapter 5). Finally, "letting go" may seem to be an issue primarily for parents approaching the empty nest. In reality, however, "letting go" starts as soon as we become parents (chapter 6).

This volume of LIFESEARCH will help parents develop principles and skills for parenting. Thinking about principles which guide us in parenting can help us to decide on appropriate strategies to use. Recognizing principles can help us refrain from actions that harm children or that divert us from being the kind of parents we want to be. Furthermore, principles are more than specific techniques to use with children of

a certain age, only to be dropped when children reach the next stage. Principles guide us in selecting, discarding, or rejecting parenting techniques throughout our children's lives. Being a loving parent to a college student requires parents to show love differently than when that child was a baby. However, since this study explores principles of parenting, it can be used well by parents of any age child.

In each chapter, there are skills for participants to practice together and with which to experiment at home between sessions. You may already use some of these skills as part of your "parenting repertoire." If so, you can help support others in your LIFESEARCH group. If the skill or process suggested is new, remember that it takes time to become comfortable with new actions and ways of doing things. You may wobble and wonder if you will ever get the hang of it, just as a child does when trying to ride a two-wheeler. You may wonder if it is even appropriate for you and your family. The skills and processes offered in LIFESEARCH are merely suggestive. They have worked for other parents. They may or may not work well for you or with a particular child. But by trying them, you will have a chance to see if they can be helpful tools to use. Other parents in the group can benefit from hearing about your experience in using them.

In each chapter, part of the material will be devoted to the Christian context. We believe that being a Christian parent is different from merely being a good parent. While all the implications for the Christian parent cannot be explored in each chapter, we hope that the ideas presented will act as a springboard to further study and discussion about how to be Christlike in our parenting.

Another important part of this resource focuses on the communal responsibilities of the Christian church to nurture children in our midst and in society-at-large. When children are baptized, the congregation promises to nurture the child and his or her family so that they might grow in faith. Congregations sometimes feel they have fulfilled their responsibilities if they offer a Sunday school class and worship service to those willing to "show up" at the appointed times. Each session offers LIFESEARCH groups a chance to explore how congregations might nurture children and their families beyond a few hours a week. How might congregations enlarge opportunities for Christian families during those other 166 "real life" hours a week?

An African proverb says, "It takes a whole village to raise a child." We hope that during the time of this study and beyond, you will feel that others in your LIFESEARCH group are becoming "the village," supporting you as you raise your child. We hope that you will also be a part of the village that seeks to help other participants in raising their children. We hope that your LIFESEARCH group can work together in nurturing the children in your midst— your neighborhoods, congregations, and society-at-large. There is no finer or more important work in the world!

—Cheryl Reames

Cheryl Reames is a freelance writer and teacher. She, her pastor husband, and their two sons, live in Herndon, Virginia. A member of Community of Faith United Methodist Church and a certified lab leader, she has been actively involved in the Christian education of preschoolers through middle adults. She has taught reading in the public schools. Cheryl holds degrees in elementary education and reading from Shenandoah University and in behavioral science from Scarritt College. She has a MRE from Wesley Theological Seminary.

CHAPTER ONE

SELF-IMAGE AND SELF-ESTEEM

CHECKING IN

If you have chalkboard or newsprint available, write down the reasons why persons have chosen to be a part of this group. Record this information so that you can come back to it at the end of the study to determine to what degree expectations have been met.

If the group is larger than twelve to fifteen members, ask persons to share the personal information in smaller groups of three or four. Then ask them to share expectations with the whole group.

The gathering time helps build community and encourages a climate for open and honest sharing. At this time each session you will get to know other members by sharing events of the past week.

For this first meeting be prepared to share (1) your name; (2) brief information about your family, work, and leisure activities; (3) why you have chosen to be a part of this group; and (4) the ages and interests of your child or children.

DISCUSSION POINT

What would you want your child to see?

What would you hate for your child to see?

Imagine Yourself as a Mirror

Imagine that you could hold up a mirror to yourself and your family for the last week. What would you see happening? How would you see yourself as a parent? What would the mirror reflect concerning your child or children?

Imagine yourself as a mirror. Imagine that when your child looks in the mirror, the child can see in the reflection everything you think about him or her. Imagine further that your child will use what he or she sees in the mirror to decide what he or she is worth.

Here is what two different children might see. Tamika: "I am a special person. I am smart and can do a lot of things. My dad tells his friends how hard I try on my school work. He always notices everything good I can do. I am a valuable person!"

Eric looks into the mirror and thinks: "My dad can't stand me. He is always telling me to get lost so he can hear the TV. He thinks I am stupid and dumb. He always says, 'Dummy, why can't you remember what I tell you?' He must be sorry he got me, because I am worthless."

DISCUSSION POINT

What do you think about self-esteem?

To what extent is self-esteem important? In what ways?

Self-worth or self-esteem is what persons think of themselves. It is the value persons place on themselves. Self-image is an important part of self-worth and self-esteem. Self-image is the mental picture of persons that determines what those persons think they are worth. Persons with low self-worth, low self-esteem, or a poor self-image think they are not as good as others. Persons with high self-esteem think they are worthy and have good opinions of themselves.

Persons with high self-esteem have confidence and expect to succeed. Persons with high self-esteem respect themselves as well as others. These persons are able to make friends, to learn, to work toward achieving their potential. Self-esteem helps children and adults feel happy with themselves. It also helps them cope with setbacks and disappointments.

Persons with low self-esteem do not feel able to handle new situations, to trust their own ideas, or to feel able to deal with life. According to James M. Harris, author of *You and Your Child's Self-Esteem* (Warner Books, 1989), low self-esteem can lead to physical disorders, disease, drinking and alcoholism, drug abuse, depression, suicide, and teenage sexual promiscuity and pregnancy. According to E. Kent Hayes, author of *Why Good Parents Have Bad Kids: How to Make Sure That Your Child Grows Up Right*, writes, ". . . there is one personality trait common to most kids who get in trouble: a very poor self-image" (Doubleday, 1989; page 107).

WRITTEN REFLECTION

On a separate piece of paper or newsprint sheet write characteristics of a positive or a negative self-image that you see in your child or children.

Ingredients of Self-Esteem

James M. Harris says that two ingredients contribute to self-esteem: love and capability. Children need to feel without a doubt that they are loved by their parents and other persons who are significant in their lives. They also need to feel confident that they have many abilities. (We will talk more about capability in chapter 6, "Letting Go.")

WRITTEN REFLECTION

Again on a separate piece of paper or sheet of newsprint, list the capabilities of your child or children.

Self-esteem grows from the relationships a child has within the family and with other significant persons in his or her life. What parents and family say to a child and how they treat the child have much to do with whether the child develops high or low self-esteem.

According to Harris, self-esteem develops through a process called a "mirror-image concept" or the "looking-glass self" (*You and Your Child's Self-Esteem*; pages 11-12). Children view themselves as they think important adults, such as their parents, view them. Children become the "mirror-image" of what the parent and other persons act as if the children might be. Positive expectations seem to develop and enhance self-esteem. Negative reflections and comments seem to detract from self-esteem. If we see love, we assume we are lovable. If we see displeasure, we assume we are displeasing.

Lowering Self-Esteem

Parents too easily communicate or reflect negative images. Parents may feel stressed from a job or lack of a job, from financial worries, or from the lack of emotional support. Parents may feel overwhelmed by demands of parenting and feel that they don't have the energy or time or necessary knowledge to deal with the demands. Parents may be short-tempered with children, spend little time with them, and criticize them because they want the best for them. When parents are overstressed, they tend to focus on the negative. But children see a grouchy parent and think, "My parent is grouchy because I am bad." Or, "My parent complains so much because I can't do anything right." Parents lower self-esteem when they reject, criticize, dislike, or ignore the child. Parents can't totally avoid sending messages that hurt a child's self-esteem, but they can consciously work to help the child build a strong self-image and to refrain from comments and behaviors that lower self-esteem.

Building a Strong Self-Image

Parents communicate love and acceptance of the child when they focus on what is positive about the child. They strengthen the child's self-esteem when they praise and listen to the child.

Parents also build a child's self-esteem when they focus on the child's strengths.

GROUP INTERACTION

Give these directions to group members: Find a partner. Imagine that your partner is your child. For one minute, express verbally what you find positive about your child. Be specific. Reverse roles.

DISCUSSION POINT

What would happen if you tried this exercise at home with your child?

DISCUSSION POINT

To what extent do you think these four ideas are workable?

BIBLE STUDY

Use these Scriptures as God's mirror to view yourself.

What does God see as your worth?

Do you see that worth? Why or why not?

How do you see yourself as the image of God?

What qualities of God do you see in yourself as a person? as a parent?

How do you see that you are being transformed into God's image in ever-greater degrees?

Here are some ways you can help strengthen your child's self-esteem:

1. Think of what you find positive about your child. Find ways to tell the child: "You tried hard to do a good job." "Your smile makes me feel happy." "You show me things I hadn't noticed." Praise what your child does that you like. Be specific, rather than general, so that the child can identify with the "reflection" you are giving. "I liked how quickly you came when I called," not "You are a good kid."

2. Eliminate negative comments: "You are so slow that you always make me late." "You are a pig and your room is a pig-pen." "You'll probably be a juvenile delinquent like your friends."

3. Increase your child's self-esteem by increasing your own self-esteem. Work on raising your own self-esteem by concentrating on your strengths. Admitting honestly when you did a good job or when you exhibit positive qualities is not conceited. It shows that you value yourself in a healthy way. You can say, "I worked hard to get that account." (Not "I am smarter than those dummies in my office.") You can say, "I am pleased that I held my temper." (You don't have to say, "I am better than that mother who lost her temper at the ball game.")

4. Model good self-esteem for your child. Refrain from making derogatory comments about yourself. Praise yourself for your good qualities. (This includes accepting compliments graciously.) Use self-praise to model good self-esteem for your child.

The Bible and Image

Read the following Bible passages: Genesis 1:27; Psalm 8; and 2 Corinthians 3:18.

As many parenting books today talk of self-image, self-esteem, and self-concept, so the Bible also talks about the importance of image. Dictionaries define *image* as a likeness or imitation of something, a visual representation, and a person who bears a strong resemblance to another.

Two ideas can be important when Christian parents are thinking of building the self-esteem first in themselves and then in the child. The first might be called "God-esteem," meaning the esteem that God holds for us, and "God-image," meaning seeing the image of God in the self.

DISCUSSION POINT

What do you think of these concepts of "God-esteem" and "God-image"?

To what extent are these concepts helpful to your situation? In what ways?

How would you answer this question?

GROUP INTERACTION

How can you enhance your child's self-esteem?

Who are important people who affect your child's self-esteem? How can you help them treat your child in a way that will enhance self-esteem?

What ways do you use to help your child feel good about himself or herself? Share your ideas with the group.

GROUP INTERACTION

Help participants recognize that real change in habits takes time and patience to develop. They should not expect instant results when they try a new skill or process. They may also get better results if they introduce changes gradually than if they make huge changes all at once for a week and then change to a different skill or process each week. Not all suggestions will fit all situations. Persons should select carefully those that will best fit their families.

The verses you read apply to your child also. <u>How can you hold up a mirror so that your child sees how much worth God thinks the child has? How can you hold a mirror up to your children so that they will see God's image in themselves and grow ever stronger in that image? What can you say and do so that the child recognizes the qualities of God in himself or herself?</u>

<u>How would it change your parenting if your child constantly wore a sign around her neck saying: "I am the image of God" or "I am just a little lower than God"? How would you relate to your child if you had a sign on your hand that said: "I am the image of God and I should reflect it"?</u>

Explore the Issues

Recognizing that you are not the only person who has contributed to your child's level of self-esteem, measure on a scale of 1 (lowest) to 10 (highest) what you think your child's self-esteem is at this point. Tell a partner one or more ways that self-esteem has affected your child's life.

In smaller groups of two or three persons, practice these skills. Pick the skill or skills that you think might best fit your situation. Then try them out with your family this week.

1. Practice seeing others' strengths. Give compliments to the group members on either side of you. Practice receiving their compliments graciously by responding with an affirmation—whether you agree with the compliment or not. ("Thank you, I have always liked the color of my eyes, too." "Thank you, I am glad to hear that you think so.") Praise your child's strengths at least three times each day this week.

2. Practice modeling self-esteem. Think of one strength you have or something about yourself that pleases you. Tell the group. ("I tried hard and got here on time." "I complimented both my children today without knowing it was good for their self-esteem." "I showed courage by saying I'd lead this study tonight.") Model for your child(ren) an appreciation for your own strengths at least twice a day this week.

3. Practice reflecting God's image. Think of a way you reflect God's image. Tell that to the group. ("God is patient. I was patient with the receptionist today." "God is the Creator. I shared God's ability to create by having a child." "God is steadfast and faithful. I never give up on my children even when they do wrong.") Reflect God's image back to your child at least once a day. ("God cares for people. You were caring when Jamal was feeling sad today.")

DISCUSSION POINT

What might Andre have seen in the self-image mirror that has been held up to him? Do you think Andre can see the image of God in himself? Why or why not? Do you think Andre can recognize the image of God in others?

WRITTEN REFLECTION

Write down your reflections on these questions. Then discuss them with one or two other persons.

CHECKING IN

GROUP INTERACTION

Have participants who wish to do so exchange phone numbers in order to support one another during the week.

You may wish to record phone numbers on the last page of this study guide.

Self-Image and God's Image in a Wider Context

Andre is 15 years old. He never knew his father. His mother is on welfare and has never had enough money to provide adequate food, clothing, or shelter for Andre and his brothers and sisters. Andre had learning problems and was not able to do well in school. He is now living in a neighborhood where drugs are bought and sold and gunfire is commonplace. Drugs and crime seem the only way he can support himself.

What might be the responsibility of the individual Christian or a congregation to help persons like Andre in the community and the nation develop a strong self-image? to see the image of God in themselves? How could you individually, your congregation, and your denomination do that? How do you do that with your own child's friends?

Hold a mirror up to the group. How do you see the group? How is the group reflecting the image of God? How might the group need to shine up the mirror in order to do a better job of reflecting God's image?

Establish a Covenant for Mutual Support

Hopefully you and the other group participants will want to support one another with concerns being explored during this study. Discuss your responses to these questions with the group.

• How would you like for the group to help support you during this study?

• Whom can you help support this week?

• How will you provide support?

• How could the group help you improve your ability to see God's image within yourself? How could the group boost your self-esteem? How could they help you better reflect God's image to your child? Share an idea about this with the group.

• How could you enhance the self-esteem of one or more group members? Try to hold a positive mirror up to at least one person every time the group meets during the study.

• After persons share the ways they need support, join hands with one another and pledge the following covenant to one another: "I will support you as best I can. Unless you give me permission, I will not share with others the family concerns you have shared with me. I will pray for you and your family, and I ask you to pray for me and my family."

Pray Together

Pray together as a group. Use this prayer or one of your own.

O God, you have made us in your image. As parents, we seek to reflect your image. Teach us to help our children see your image in themselves and to help them grow more nearly in your likeness. As we grow in your image, we seek to support one another. We bring these concerns before you now. (Pray aloud or silently for each of the prayer needs and concerns.) *We bring our prayers in Jesus' name. Amen.*

WORSHIP

Ask for any additional prayer concerns that might not have been mentioned at the beginning of the session.

CHAPTER TWO

DISCIPLINE

CHECKING-IN

Deepen your group's identity and feelings for one another by sharing responses to the following:

—What has happened in your life in the past week that you want to share with the group?

—What is coming up in the next week that you want the group to know about?

—What happened during last week as you worked to hold a positive, loving mirror up for your children and yourself?

DISCUSSION POINT

Invite group members to respond to this question. Note responses on chalkboard or newsprint, if available.

Discipline: What Is It?

What's the first word that pops into your mind when you hear the word *discipline*?

Perhaps your word was *punishment, penalty, self-control,* or it may have been *headache, pain,* or *problem*. Many persons think of discipline as something negative, something parents have to apply when their children do not behave as they are supposed to.

DISCUSSION POINT

What are the goals you want to accomplish by using discipline? (For example: Keep the house intact; raise happy, well-behaved children.)

What principles do you use to guide you in selecting a system or method of discipline? (For example: I want to enhance self-esteem, treat the child in a loving manner, preserve the child's creativity and individuality, enhance mutual respect.)

Although at least one dictionary classifies that meaning as "obsolete," discipline can also refer to instruction. Discipline can be training, such as the training musicians or athletes adhere to in order to maximize their performance. When teachers refer to "good discipline," they usually mean orderly conduct.

Punishment vs. Discipline

Punishment includes spanking and aversive consequences: physical pain, grounding, isolation, loss of privileges. When it comes to discipline, a problem with punishment alone is that it does not teach the child what he or she is to do, only what he or she isn't to do. Heavy reliance on punishment leads to feelings of guilt, resentment, and hostility. Physical punishments such as hitting teaches unintended lessons, such as: to hit, you just have to be bigger, stronger, and in charge.

Rewards, on the other hand, direct the child to the behavior that is desired and make it likely that good behavior will happen again. Rewards can include praise, time with parents, a fun family activity, a toy, a sticker, or some other item or privilege. A reward is different from a bribe. A bribe is something given or promised ahead of time for *not* doing something. A reward is given afterwards for doing something right.

WRITTEN REFLECTION

Consider whether you more often bribe or reward. What differences between the two do you see in your family? Write your reflection to this question in the space below:

GROUP INTERACTION

Discuss your reflection with a person other than your spouse.

In parenting, it is probably impossible to avoid punishment totally. However, parents can remember that positive rewards lead to positive behavior, and positive behavior leads to and strengthens self-esteem.

How Much Discipline?

Parents choose many styles of discipline, from almost no rules and total freedom, to strict control over almost every aspect in a child's life. The right amount of discipline shows a child that the parent cares what happens to the child. Too much control makes the child feel that the parent lacks trust in the child. Children need reasonable, consistent guidance and controls on their behavior until they are mature enough to develop self-control. Effective discipline helps a child become well-adjusted.

Toward Self-Discipline

Discipline can be viewed as positive. We feel positive when we have used good self-discipline—when we exercise regularly, when we have healthy teeth because we take care of them, when we learn because we want to, when we finish a project we have started. Children, too, need to learn that discipline can be rewarding. They need to become disciplined within themselves, not because discipline is imposed on them. You want your children to behave as well when you are not home as when you are, when they are away from your influence as well as when you are in the room with them. Telling children sensible reasons for behaving in certain ways and refraining from harmful behaviors helps children understand that behaving in appropriate ways is more than not getting caught. ("We drive at the posted speed even when no police are around because driving at or under the speed limit is safer than speeding.")

Rules and Consequences

Rules can help a family function smoothly. The best rules are probably made before behavior becomes a problem, as a preventive rather than a corrective measure. Rules should be clearly stated and understood. Consequences should follow when a rule is violated. A consequence can be made a part of the rule. That way parents do not always have to come up with a new penalty. Children may look on rules without consequences as simply suggestions. When there are no clear rules, parents have to fight issues daily or plead for the child to follow expectations.

GROUP INTERACTION

With one or two partners, practice formulating one or two rules and the natural or logical consequences that you might use with your own child or children. Then discuss with your partner, <u>did the rule seem appropriate? Were the consequences logical and reasonable?</u> Try using some rules and logical consequences with your family this week.

Children can have an important voice in setting rules and consequences. It often works well to ask a child what might be a fair punishment for a particular situation. The child will often suggest a punishment that is harsher than the one a parent might have chosen. You might ask the child to suggest two or three possible consequences and then the parent can pick one. If the child suggests silly consequences, the parent can state that the child does not seem ready to set consequences and that the parent will do it.

BEFORE NEXT TIME

Try this at home before the next session! Be ready to share next time how asking your child to suggest a fair consequence worked.

Some parents ground children, particularly teenagers, for any misbehavior. Such punishment is often ineffective because it does not help the child or teen recognize logical consequences or distinguish between minor misbehavior and major misbehavior. Length of grounding may be the only difference between punishment for talking too long on the phone and for driving while drinking.

Logical or natural consequences are what happen as a result of the child's actions. It can be effective to use logical consequences as part of rule setting or in place of punishment. For example, if the child or teen does not put dirty clothes in the proper place, the logical consequence could be that the child would have to wear dirty clothes or wash them. Doing the yard work alone the next time could be the consequence for "forgetting" to show up to help.

Children may have to wait until lunch to eat if they fail to get up on time. If children are late for school, logically they would take consequences from the teacher, rather than receive a lecture or punishment from the parent. Some benefits of using logical consequences are that the parent and child can more easily avoid yelling, physical pain, nagging, resentment, and lectures.

DISCUSSION POINT

What natural consequences might damage a child?

What natural consequences might affect a parent more than the child?

As a part of discipline, parents would not, of course, choose to allow the natural consequences if they would be damaging to the child. A parent might also choose a related consequence if the natural consequence would affect the parent more than it would affect the child.

BIBLE STUDY

The Bible and Discipline

While the Bible undoubtedly at times views discipline as punishment—and sometimes very harsh punishment, the New Testament focuses on the educational side of discipline.

DISCUSSION POINT

What do you think it means to correct with gentleness? How can some methods "provoke children to anger"? What is wrong with methods that create anger within children?

Read Ephesians 6:1-24, Colossians 3:20-21, and 2 Timothy 2:24-25.

DISCUSSION POINT

What are some methods of discipline that would violate the Golden Rule if you used them? What are ways you appreciate being informed that your behavior, speech, actions, work, or other habits need to be improved? How would your children feel if you would correct their behavior, speech, actions, work, or other habits in ways that you would appreciate being treated?

DISCUSSION POINT

When have you suspended a rule? What resulted?

DISCUSSION POINT

What is your reaction to what Dolores Curran says about discipline, behavior, and relationships?

BIBLE STUDY

Read The Golden Rule in Matthew 7:12 and Luke 6:31.

Discipline and Flexibility

In a family some rules may apply to individuals, some to family members of a certain age, and some to special circumstances. Sometimes rules get suspended. The question is, <u>will it destroy discipline if you bend or suspend the rules occasionally?</u> Flexibility is important because it can help the family function more smoothly. It helps children see that special occasions or special circumstances sometimes need flexibility.

Relationships Are Important

Dolores Curran, author of *Stress and the Healthy Family* (HarperPaperbacks, 1985), suggests that families should work to develop relationships. Curran states: "Discipline is a tool used to establish and correct behaviors. When relationships are healthy, behaviors tend to be healthy. When relationships are not healthy, the best disciplinary techniques available will not be effective in establishing positive behaviors" (page 135). She says of families, "When they can communicate and listen to each other, they are already offsetting situations which require discipline. When they affirm and support one another, respect and trust one another, and have fun together, they are building a family that doesn't have to focus on discipline as a way of existing without stress" (page 135).

The Christian Parent and Discipline

The very core of the Christian gospel is grace—God's love, freely given—not because we deserve it, but because God is "gracious" and chooses to give it. Through the whole of the Bible, God's love shows qualities of responsibility for, devotion to, and knowledge of God's people. Many words are used in various translations of the Bible to express aspects of God's love. Some of those words are steadfast love, loving kindness, loyalty, and mercy. If you are interested, look up some Bible passages such as Psalm 31:21, Psalm 33:5, and Psalm 36:5.

Throughout the Bible, we can see God's steadfast love remaining steadfast for God's children. God's children did not always do what was right. Sometimes they strayed very far from what God wanted and expected from them. Their actions often caused God grief and pain. But God never gave up on them. Even when they were doing what they knew was wrong, God's children in the Bible knew God's love for them never wavered. Our challenge is to discipline with grace so that our children recognize our steadfast love, loving kindness, loyalty, and mercy.

GROUP DISCUSSION

What does it mean to love a child even when the child knowingly does wrong?

How can you help your child(ren) experience steadfast love even when you discipline them?

How can you put mercy, loving kindness, loyalty, and steadfast love into action as you discipline?

GROUP INTERACTION

With a partner from the group, share two feelings you have about discipline in relation to your children. <u>Why might you feel that way?</u> Share one question you have about discipline. Suggest a possible answer to your partner's question about discipline. Share with the group a thought you have about discipline.

GROUP INTERACTION

Discipline in a Wider Context

Roleplay one or more of these situations, showing how persons might act as individual parents or friends or as a church board:

(A) Delia and Bob are both Sunday school teachers at First Church. When children misbehave in Bob's class, he makes them stand out in the church hall and memorize Bible verses till the end of Sunday school. When children misbehave in Delia's class, she questions them and tries to understand why the children are misbehaving. Then she goes back to the lesson. <u>What would you suggest to these teachers about discipline?</u> <u>What kind of discipline should be used in Sunday school?</u>

(B) Carolyn and her five-year-old daughter Molly were shopping. When Molly kept playing with a toy display after Carolyn had told her several times to stop, Carolyn twisted Molly's arm and started loudly calling her names. You turn a corner and see what is happening. Carolyn is your friend from church. <u>As a church member and friend, what do you do? What should the church be doing to help parents know appropriate ways to discipline children? What should the community do?</u>

DISCUSSION POINT

Many parents now provide little discipline for their children. Others provide inconsistent punishments based on how much the child is annoying the parent at the moment. <u>What happens to a family when parents do not provide appropriate discipline? What happens to a community when parents do not provide appropriate discipline? What happens to the society? What can a community of faith or a church congregation do about what is happening? What can you as an individual do?</u>

CHECKING IN

You may want to ask some persons why they gave the answers they did. Ask for suggestions about how the group might better meet the needs of participants.

Check the Group's Discipline

Look at the discipline of the group. Do any rules or guidelines need to be made, changed, or eliminated to help the group function more smoothly? for the group to better serve its purpose? If so, what are they? What self-discipline might you or others apply to get more from the study and the group?

WORSHIP

Pray Together

As you close this session, share specific prayer concerns with one another. Record those prayer concerns in the space below.

Pray together as a group. Use this prayer or one of your own. Be sure to include prayers for the concerns mentioned by your group.

O God, we know you love us even when we do wrong. Help us love our children even when they misbehave. Teach us how to instruct and discipline with love. We bring these concerns before you now in Jesus' name. Amen.

CHAPTER THREE

STRESSES

CHECKING IN

Examples: "Our mobile has been hanging quietly." "Our mobile has been blown wildly around by too many pressures."

Imagine yourself and your children as part of a hanging mobile. Describe to the group the kind of balance found in your "hanging mobile." What "winds" of stress have come along during the past week and twisted your family's "strings?" What is coming up in the next week that you want the group to know about? What happened during the past week in relation to what we have been talking about in the last couple of weeks? How did asking your child to suggest a fair consequence work? What concerns and joys do you wish to share so that other group members can pray with you today and during the week to come?

Families and Stress

You've finally finished that lengthy and ever-changing "To Do" list. As you sit down to relax, your spouse walks in the door and announces that the car, which just had a repair that cost over three hundred dollars, has broken down again; so your family can't drive the after-school car pool tomorrow. The stresses of family life never seem to stop.

GROUP INTERACTION

Ask group members to name one of their biggest stresses if they are comfortable in doing so. As each member shares, ask if anyone in the group can suggest help.

All families have stresses, and many of those are generally the same from family to family, according to Dolores Curran, author of *Stress and the Healthy Family* (HarperPaperbacks, 1985). Curran says that families worry about money, how to cope with time, how to deal with children. But there is a difference in the way some families cope with pressures. Curran says: "Some learn to control family stress; others allow stress to control their family lives" (page 6).

GROUP INTERACTION

Ask persons to think about how calm or stressful life was in the families in which they grew up. Invite them to position themselves on an imaginary line across the room, from "completely serene" to "absolutely chaotic."

Ask: Did your family seek to display more calm to the outside world than it really experienced?

DISCUSSION POINT

To what extent do you agree with this statement?

How does the stress affecting one family member affect others in your family?

WRITTEN REFLECTION

How has distress been displayed within your family during the last month?

Part of the problem may come from the way we think of the marriage ceremony. We may ignore the "for richer, for poorer, in sickness and in health" portion and concentrate instead on the romance and pageantry of the occasion. We think families are not supposed to have stresses. When we think our home is always supposed to be calm, peaceful, and without stress—and we see it isn't—we can feel even more pressure and stress because we feel great guilt. We think we have failed.

Many stresses families face, Curran suggests, come from the way work and school patterns are set up. Other stresses come from attitudes and expectations of the community, the church, or of individuals and families. Problems from all these areas create stress on family members. In turn, the pressures that create family stress at home show up as stresses on society. Stress on one family member affects all the persons in the family.

The first thing parents need to do to cope with family stresses in a healthy way is to recognize that family stresses are normal and to be expected. The goal is not to eliminate stress completely, but to learn to handle stresses in a competent manner.

Transform Your Image of Stress

Stress can be good. Positive stress—called *eustress* (Curran, page 12) is stimulating. It helps us get our work done. It gives us the drive to excel and do our best. With good stress, an individual has a feeling of some control. Distress is what happens when conditions get out of control. You can name several symptoms of distress in your family. You may feel like screaming, "I'm going to run away!" or "Everybody just leave me alone!" You are constantly feeling, "I'll never get everything done." Your children seem to spend more time whining and fighting, and complaining more of headaches and stomachaches. The real problem with stress comes when you feel that stress cannot be controlled. Whether stress results in excellence or in distress results from what a person chooses to do in response to the stress.

On a separate piece of paper or newsprint, identify symptoms of distress in your family.

Change your vocabulary to focus on the positive. Instead of *problems*, face *challenges* and *opportunities*. Instead of thinking, "I'll never make it," think "Sure, I've got the strength to handle this!" Point out the new skills that have come to family members because of stress and how those skills might be of help now and in the future. "I learned more about learning disabilities and was able to suggest some resources to a new friend I recently met." "When unexpected company phoned from the next town, we discovered how well we could clean up the living room in fifteen minutes—so now we get it cleaned up that fast all the time." By dealing with stresses, you gain strength and skills to face additional stress (Curran, page 2).

Become Stress-Sleuths and Stress-Solvers

DISCUSSION POINT

What future stresses can you predict in your family's life? How might you prepare to cope with them?

As a family, try to figure out what factors are causing various stresses. Do you forget dates of events or appointments until the last minute? Use a calendar to write down all family events and appointments. Store announcement sheets with the calendar so that you can find them easily for more information. Write dates on the calendar as you read the school newsletter, the church bulletin, the Little League calendar. Does one child always misplace her shoes and make the family late by having to look for them? Teach the child to take the shoes off only in a certain place. Penalize her when they are found elsewhere and reward family members for discovering them ahead of time. Be creative in finding solutions to stress.

Stresses change as members of a family grow and develop. Some stresses are fairly predictable, such as a new baby, a move, or a change in jobs or schools. Families can handle such stresses better if they prepare ahead for coping. Send for information about a new town ahead of time. Read books that tell what stresses families might expect when a new sibling arrives or a grandparent dies. Plan for everyday stresses. Allow extra time when you know you might get caught in traffic. Have an extra box of cake mix and a can of frosting on hand for times when you don't discover until after dinner that your child volunteered to take cup cakes the next day.

Eliminate Unreasonable Expectations

DISCUSSION POINT

What are other examples of unrealistic expectations placed upon children?

Some stress comes from unrealistic expectations. Recognize children's limitations. Try not to push them beyond what is reasonable for them to do or achieve. Recognize what you expect. What you say you expect may not be what you really expect. ("I expect him to make the grades he is capable of making" can mean "I expect him to make all A's." That may not be reasonable.) Don't push children into situations for which they are not ready, but do let them do for themselves what they can do.

The fact that our culture and its values are changing so quickly causes major stress to families. For example children

DISCUSSION POINT

What are other examples of outside "shoulds?"

DISCUSSION POINT

How aware are you of your personal level of stress?

beg for advertised clothing and toys that may be beyond the reach of the family budget or outside the values that parents want to teach. Schools and churches expect a certain level of involvement, but work requirements and family demands often interfere. Well-meaning persons and authorities preach what we "should" do. One way to cope with these pressures is for parents and families to decide their own "shoulds." As far as possible, they can decide what they can and will do. Families cannot follow all "shoulds" even if those "shoulds" are good ideas. Families need to set their own healthy limits without feeling guilty. Only the persons within a family know what they can and cannot manage.

Recognize priorities and eliminate other activities. Do your children take music lessons because they love it, because you think it is good for them, or because all the other children in your neighborhood take music lessons? Your family cannot do everything. Talk about what is most important to you as a family and as individuals. Try to adjust your life to accommodate priorities of family members and eliminate what is unimportant.

Stress affects individuals and families in a variety of ways. Stress can result in divorce, depression, abuse, bankruptcy, and crime. Stress can cause physical illness. Dr. Peter G. Hanson, a physician and author of *Stress for Success* (Doubleday, 1989) says that eighty percent of all illnesses are related to stress. Heart attacks, infections, ulcers, injuries, alcoholism, drug addiction, and smoking have all been blamed on stress. Stress can also cause headaches, insomnia, fatigue, poor concentration, eating disorders, depression, and anxiety. Even children begin to develop symptoms of stress-related disorders and illnesses. Signs of stress in children can also be headaches, stomachaches, eating problems, sleeping problems, poor grades, nail-biting, bedwetting, or a variety of other symptoms. Take an occasional stress check to see if your family members are showing the effects of stress.

Select Healthy Ways to Cope

DISCUSSION POINT

Ask the group members to look over the suggestions for coping with stress listed in the text. Then ask them to pick several and suggest ways they personally might put them into action.

Healthy and unhealthy ways exist to cope with stress. Some persons handle stress by blaming others, or by turning to smoking, alcohol, drugs (prescription or illegal), fatty foods, overdosing on television, and overspending on credit cards. Instead of eliminating or reducing stress, these methods lead to more stress. You can choose whether you will emerge from a stress more confident, more competent, and with greater health or whether the stress will conquer you by taking your energy, your health, and your happiness. You can learn to use stress to your benefit.

There are three ways to know if stress is beginning to overwhelm you, says Dr. Hanson. One way is by the physical sensations in your body. A second is by listening to or asking your family or friends. A third is a medical checkup, since physical and chemical changes in the body can occur as a result of stress.

Healthy ways of coping with stress can make you stronger as a family and as individuals. Find what relieves stress for each family member. It may be physical exercise, playing games, reading, listening to music, or talking. Learn new ways to cope with stress, such as muscle relaxation exercises, mental imaging, list making and selecting priorities, roleplaying "what-ifs," or meditation. Teach your children how to deal with various types of stresses through a variety of means. Take time for rest and recreation as a family and as individuals. You can strengthen family relationships, build happy memories, and teach your children healthy ways of coping that can become lifelong habits.

Some people cope with stress by withdrawing. Some cope by nonstop talking. Recognize that each person will have his or her own way to cope with stress. Allow for individuality. Teach your children to share feelings without denying or belittling another person's feelings. It is okay for family members to feel differently about events that cause stress. What is exciting to one person can be draining and exhausting for another person. You can still love and appreciate one another even though you think and feel differently about ideas, events, persons, and stresses.

Stresses seem greater when persons are rigid and inflexible. Children may have a hard time being flexible and adaptable. A child may refuse to wear any jeans that are not a certain size, color, and style. One fast-food place may be the only one where a particular child may be happy. Your spouse may want the car parked in the driveway a certain way. Try to find out the reasons that family members seem inflexible on certain issues. A child may find change scary. A teen may want to wear other clothes but find himself ostracized when he wears them. The neighbor children may run their bikes into a car that is an inch too near the sidewalk. Try to work out what family members can be flexible about. Encourage adaptability when appropriate.

Seek Support With Stresses

Help in coping with stress is becoming available to families. Some companies are beginning to have counselors on staff to help employees deal with family problems that affect their work performance. Some schools offer parenting courses because they recognize that what happens in the home affects the performance of children in school. Schools may also offer guidance counselors and other resources to help children cope with stress. Some churches work to help strengthen families by focusing on ministering to families within their homes, not just at church. Some community institutions, such as churches, community colleges, women's centers, and so forth offer classes in parenting and family issues. Find or develop and use support systems: friends, family, neighbors, church, professionals, and those in similar situations.

BIBLE STUDY

The Bible and Stresses

Read Matthew 6:25-34 and Matthew 11:28-30.

Jesus told his followers not to worry. When you are a parent today, it is hard to keep from worrying. The economy is bad. Jobs are not secure. Violence increases. Your children may have learning problems. Family members may have handicaps or health problems. What, you wonder, could Jesus have been thinking when he said, "Don't worry about your life"? But Jesus did know that people carry heavy burdens and he invited us to bring those burdens to him.

DISCUSSION POINT

What do you think Jesus is suggesting about priorities in our life?

Do any of your stresses come because of misplaced priorities?

Jesus carried heavy burdens of stress, too. Yet he recognized that worry only increases stress. It does not reduce it. It has been estimated that three-quarters of the things we worry *might* happen do not happen. Jesus did not tell us to stop working or abandon our responsibilities. He suggested that we take care of today the things we can do something about today. Tomorrow we can take care of what we can manage tomorrow.

There are times in our lives when we may have to worry about where we will get the food for our next meal or how we are going to buy needed clothes for our children. But at other times we put pressures on ourselves and our families because of what we or they want: designer jeans, the most popular athletic shoes, or a newer car or TV. When so much energy is spent trying to get ahead or keeping up with what others have, we lose sight of what matters most in life—spending time with friends and family, putting our trust in God instead of our own efforts, resting our bodies when we need it. Putting priority on relationships with our families and with God and less emphasis on worldly values can help reduce some of the stresses in our life.

BIBLE STUDY

What do these passages say to you personally? Share with group members some images of God that you think would be comforting or some Bible verses that you know that tell of God or Jesus as a comforter.

BEFORE NEXT TIME

DISCUSSION POINT

If many group members feel the same stress, what could the group do to help relieve the stress for themselves and their families as well as for other parents and children?

CHECKING IN

WORSHIP

Pray together as a group. Use this prayer or one of your own. Be sure to include prayer for the joys and concerns mentioned at the beginning of the session.

God—A Source of Rest and Restoration

Read Psalm 23; Psalm 57:1; and Matthew 23:37.

God can be a source of rest and restoration. Throughout the Bible, there are images of God as a protector, a comforter, a source of rest and strength to endure life's storms. Psalm 23 tells that the Lord restores our soul. Psalm 57:1 tells that we can take refuge in the shadow of God's wings until the storms pass. The message of the Bible is that God gives us the strength and power to endure difficult times and to overcome them.

This week look for Bible verses that provide images of God that are restful, strengthening, comforting, and restoring. Try mental imaging each day to help relieve and cope with stress. Have your children try it with you if they are old enough.

Pressures in a Wider Context

How does your church stress families? Does it put out expectations (silently or otherwise) that put extra stress on parents and families? How does your church support families? Does it always provide childcare during meetings and services? Does it provide a welcoming atmosphere so that families with small children feel free to participate in dinners, activities, and worship? Or do families feel they must rush out at the first whimper from the baby or whine from an older child?

Check the Group's Stress Level

What pressures does the group seem to be feeling at this moment? What pressures do you feel from the group? What pressures do you put on the group? Is there stress in the group? Why? What can be done about it? How is the group helping you with family stresses?

Pray Together

O God, we feel stresses from many sources. You invite us to bring our stresses to you. Thank you for the help you give us to cope with the problems and burdens we bear. Thank you that we can provide support to one another so that we can make others' stresses easier for them to bear. We bring these concerns before you now, in Jesus' name. Amen.

CHAPTER FOUR

DEALING WITH CONFLICTS

CHECKING IN

1. Imagine each of your family members as a nation. How would you describe the "international relations" that have occurred during the past week?

2. What is coming up in the next week that you want the group to know about?

3. What Bible images of God did you find helpful since last time?

The Christian and Conflict

As much as we may long for peace in our families, conflict always arises. An important task for parents is teaching children how to deal with conflict in healthy, nondestructive ways. The goal for a Christian should be to solve conflicts and differences in a Christlike manner. That means facing the fact that conflicts exist, that persons have feelings, and that nobody should have to stuff down feelings and act as if everything is okay when it is really not.

Solving conflicts as Christians means working to resolve difficulties with fairness, with regard to the dignity of all persons involved, and with as little harm as possible. Christians should work to resolve conflicts in such a way that, as far as possible, everybody wins.

DISCUSSION POINT

If you held in your hand an expandable duffle bag, how full would you have stuffed it with feelings this past week? To what size would the duffle bag have to expand? To what size would the duffle bag have to expand in order to hold the feelings you think all your family stuffed down this past week?

Wendell claims he is a peacemaker. He says he and his wife Elaine have never had an argument. When their two children Megan, age 10, and Andrew, age 8, begin to argue, Wendell is able to stop their squabble with one look. <u>What do you think Wendell, Elaine, Megan, and Andrew have learned about conflict? What could you suggest to the family to help them deal with conflicts in a healthy way?</u>

DISCUSSION POINT

Ask the group to read and discuss this case study in connection with the material presented in the earlier paragraph.

Model Problem-Solving

The first way to teach children how to deal with conflict is for parents to learn and use good methods to handle their own conflicts. When children see parents fighting and yelling or using violent means to solve their own problems and con-

DISCUSSION POINT

What method for managing conflict do your children see you modeling?

flicts, children will come to believe that how the parent handles conflict is *the* way to use. You teach your child good ways to manage conflict and solve problems when you use methods that preserve the dignity of all parties in the conflict. By your actions and your words, you can show your children that there is a better way than screaming, fighting, and rage.

DISCUSSION POINT

Ask the group to read and discuss this case study in connection with the material presented in the above paragraph.

What are your thoughts about the way Darlene and her family approach their conflicts? What have they learned about problem solving?

Darlene yells a lot when conflicts come up in her household. She yells how she feels about the situation, what she thinks, and ways she thinks the problems can be solved. Her children yell right back at her and at each other. Darlene listens as they yell what they feel and think. They yell how they think the differences could be solved. They continue until they reach a solution. When they finish, everyone seems happy and satisfied that they have reached a good conclusion.

Control Exposure to Other Influences

Children have a constant model of unhealthy and ineffective ways to solve problems in some movies and television programs. Children constantly exposed to violent ways of handling emotions and solving conflicts will use those methods because they think that is the way it should be done. Studies are showing that children who watch more violence on television resort to violence more often than children who view less violence. Parents who want their children to learn good ways to solve conflicts are careful about the role models they allow their children to see on television, in movies, and elsewhere. Parents can also use violence and inappropriate methods of solving conflict that children see in the media to bring up discussions about more appropriate, creative, healthy ways to deal with problems.

GROUP INTERACTION

In smaller groups, look briefly at a newspaper and ask, What current examples can you find of violence used to solve conflict?

Record responses on newsprint or chalkboard, if available.

In the world today we see great evidence of hatred, anger, and hostility. Shootings, rapes, terrorist acts, threats, wars, and all manner of violence are used as solutions to conflict. As parents, we must contradict this violent message that television, movies, some books, and real life are sending our children. We must help them see that seldom does violence solve problems, conflicts, or differences. Violence can cause bigger problems. We must help them deal with anger in a better way. We must help them eliminate any hatred that starts within them. We must help children learn ways to get what they need without damaging others. Instead of blaming persons for problems, parents can help children discover real sources of problems in order to devise solutions.

DISCUSSION POINT

How well is your family doing this?

Handle Conflicts Constructively

It is good to express anger, rather than to try and contain it inside. However, some ways of expressing angry feelings are better than others. Parents need to teach children to vent frustrations on things (a pillow, a kickball, a punching bag, a flower bed that needs weeding, a room that needs vacuuming) and never on another human being, whether by kicking, hitting, swearing, yelling, or any other such means. Parents can help children recognize when they need a cooling-off time and how to take it. Parents can also help a child vent frustration by helping them learn to solve problems rather than place blame. (For example, instead of saying, "I'm angry because the teacher gave me a bad grade," say "I can get a better grade by studying harder or asking for help.") Parents should try to avoid giving in to an angry outburst. Giving in just teaches the child that angry tantrums work.

How many of your own "angry outbursts" can you recall from the past twenty-four hours? What triggered those angry outbursts?

DISCUSSION POINT

Invite persons to share their reflections about their angry outbursts. However, be sure to permit anyone who wishes to do so to "pass."

Check to see if anyone needs to work further on understanding constructive and destructive uses of anger.

Anger erupts in destructive ways because a person has not learned how to handle angry feelings and impulses. Persons do not store up anger within when they have learned how to handle their problems in effective, acceptable ways. Angry feelings often arise because of the thoughts a person thinks. ("I'm mad at him because he probably thinks I'm stupid!") Constructive anger leads a person to action. Anger over homelessness can lead persons to work to eradicate homelessness. ("Yes, I'm angry. Everybody should have a home.") For example, anger over grades can lead to better study habits. Both constructive and destructive use of anger results from what a person says internally. You can help children channel their thoughts to positive directions.

DISCUSSION POINT

What views does Victor seem to have about conflicts in families?

What are his children learning about solving problems?

What would you suggest to the family?

People handle conflicts in different ways. The authors of the Thomas-Kilmann Conflict Mode Instrument identify five responses to conflict (*Stress and the Healthy Family*; pages 41-44). Those responses are **avoidance**, **competition**, **accommodation**, **cooperation**, and **collaboration**.

Carlos and Paul are older than their 4-year-old sister Maria. When the children get into arguments about toys or television, their father Victor listens patiently and usually decides in favor of Maria, since she is younger and a girl.

DISCUSSION POINT

What family-based examples can you give for using avoidance to deal with conflict?

—competition?

—accommodation?

—compromise?

—collaboration?

Some persons use *avoidance* to deal with conflict. They act as if no conflict exists. Or they simply withdraw from the conflict. Postponing or delaying tactics can also be a form of avoiding conflict. Still other ways to avoid conflict are by sidestepping the issues or "fogging" on what the conflict is really about. When conflicts are ignored, they can mushroom. Avoiding conflicts makes it less possible to resolve them.

When persons use *competition* to resolve conflicts, there is power involved. This involves the attitude of "I win, you lose." Persons try to achieve their own wishes at the expense of others. These persons may try to seem like they are standing up for their own rights, or trying to be logical, or relying on facts to an excessive degree. Feelings are often ignored. The attitude in this situation is that there has to be a winner and a loser. Often the loser in the conflict will do something to get back at the winner.

In *accommodation* persons sacrifice their own desires and concerns to satisfy another person. The motivation can be fear of hurting another's feelings or a wish to make the other person happy, or even the wish to keep things peaceful. In this situation there is also a winner and a loser. However, the loser chooses to smooth things over doing what the other person wants.

With *compromise* each person gives up something to resolve the conflict. Kristine Miller Tomasik, in an article commenting on the various responses to conflict, says that this method is useful in dealing with minor issues needing a quick decision. However, she says, "compromise is not effective in situations which require permanent resolution because the underlying issues remain and will continue to emerge as conflicts" (*Stress and the Healthy Family*; page 44.)

Collaboration is another possible response to conflict. Tomasik thinks that this is the best method, because it explores all the issues and tries to meet everyone's needs. It requires that persons state their needs, concerns, and feelings. It requires open, honest sharing. This method takes time and involves risk, so that many people often do not try to use this method. With this method persons try to solve problems in a way that everyone wins.

Practice and Experiment

Use one or more of these case studies to practice some ways of resolving conflict. Roleplay each situation using the five ways to respond to conflict: (1) avoidance, (2) competition, (3) accommodation, (4) compromise, and (5) collaboration.

BEFORE NEXT TIME

At home this week try to identify which methods you usually use to respond to conflicts. Try some ideas suggested in this session to see which work best in various situations.

Case Study #1: Jennifer wants to use her brother Scott's bike to go to the store because her bike is broken. Scott treasures his bike and does not want anything to happen to it. Mother just wants the matter resolved quickly so that Jennifer can bring back some dinner items from the store.

Case Study #2: Tamarra just remembered she needs posterboard for a school project tomorrow. Her parent comes home with an important proposal that must be completed before work tomorrow. Tamarra has forgotten needed school supplies until the last minute at least five times before.

Case Study #3: Antonio wants to get a job after school because all his friends have jobs. His father is willing to give him extra spending money if Antonio needs it. The father values good grades and wants Antonio to spend as much time as possible on studying. The family would also need to arrange transportation and rearrange their own lives to accommodate Antonio's job.

Teach Communication Skills

Teach your child to put feelings, needs, and wants into words. Teach your child to communicate directly, rather than in an indirect manner. For example, say: "Please open my window" instead of "Can this window open?" Make it acceptable to honestly express feelings, even negative ones. Negative feelings can be expressed without disrespect or hostility. Teach your child to listen to what others are trying to express, whether verbally, through body language, or in some other way. When children can communicate in straightforward ways, they can resolve conflicts more easily.

By knowing and teaching various ways that conflicts can be handled and by fostering good communication skills, you can empower your children to face conflict in healthy ways and help them learn to recognize ineffective ways of resolving it.

Allow Children to Solve Their Conflicts

As a parent, avoid being a referee or providing an audience for your children's conflicts. Children become better at solving problems and conflicts as they practice it themselves. Refuse to be drawn into your children's conflicts, unless children are being physically harmed. Trust them to work it out. When you become a referee, you take away the chance for children to learn negotiating skills, to brainstorm solutions, to have the pleasure of working things out in a satisfactory way. Children are more inclined to work things out when they know that you cannot be drawn in

GROUP INTERACTION

Choose which title best describes your role when your children are in conflict situations. Are you referee? audience? ticket seller? promoter? or some other title? What is the most usual role for you?

Write your title on a name tag and wear it. For a few minutes meet with others with the same title. Talk about how your title affects you. What benefits or personal costs are there for you in carrying out your role?

GROUP INTERACTION

Divide the group into smaller groups of two or three persons. Have these smaller groups each identify some conflict and brainstorm twenty-five ways to solve it.

Discuss: Which solution(s) seem most usable? How might your chosen solutions affect the members of your families?

BIBLE STUDY

DISCUSSION POINT

How was Jesus wise in his view that anger and disagreements could be equal to murder?

Jesus viewed reconciliation as a priority. He believed reconciliation was so important that he placed it above what? Why do you think he valued reconciliation and peace so highly?

What current examples can you think of where truly just solutions have been created?

as an audience or a referee. The lack of parental attention lowers the children's motivation to fight with one another.

Teach children to be imaginative in thinking of ways to solve conflicts. Challenge the family to come up with twenty-five different ways to solve a conflict. The more people think of, the crazier the solutions may be—but you may find just the right solution in the more imaginative suggestions. Parents who teach children to solve problems and conflicts in a creative, fair, appropriate way are giving their children a gift that will likely be used every day for their whole lives. Resolving conflicts and finding ways to get along with others is indispensable in our world.

The Bible and Conflict Resolution

Read and reflect on Matthew 5:9 and Matthew 5:21-24.

Jesus considered peacemakers and peacemaking to be important. Peacemakers were not merely those who went around being pleasant and cheerful. They were persons who created peace in the midst of hatred. They would help reconcile persons who were alienated because of disagreements. Because we know that Jesus also believed in justice, reconciliation did not mean "just forgive and forget and act like everything is okay." Today as well as long ago, true peacemaking requires just solutions for all parties.

Conflict in a Wider Context

People are waging wars in various parts of the world. Nations try to solve disputes by bombing and killing one another. Daily media accounts tell of problems being solved violently or of persons being cheated when conflicts are being solved. On many school playgrounds during a fifteen-minute period of recess, squabbles arise and participants try to solve them by yelling, screaming, pinching, hitting, kicking, taking sides, or running to the teacher with different versions of the story.

Where do war or peace begin? When parents and children within a home cannot work out their own conflicts, will they do any better solving problems when they go to work or to school? When children see parents fighting or giving one another the silent treatment, what are they learning about resolving differences? Your family may be skilled at resolving conflicts, but what happens when family members leave home and come in contact with persons who have not learned positive, appropriate methods of solving conflicts?

DISCUSSION POINT

What is your church congregation doing to help persons learn to deal well with conflicts? What is your community doing? How can you and the group get the church and community to do more to help persons learn better ways to manage conflict and resolve differences?

Support One Another

WRITTEN REFLECTION

Ask anyone who wishes to do so to share her or his written reflections.

What ways have you found especially helpful in dealing with conflict within and outside your family? Use the space below to record your reflections.

DISCUSSION POINT

If newsprint or chalkboard is available, record resources as they are brainstormed.

What resources can you recommend to your group on problem-solving and conflict management—such as classes, books, counselors?

Check the Group's Problem-Solving

How is the group doing in solving problems or conflicts that have come up within the group? How does the group deal with conflicts or difficulties? How is it doing in dealing with feelings and needs of group members? How is it doing in helping group members find resources and methods to deal with the challenges of parenting?

✓

CHECKING IN

Persons may feel more comfortable discussing these questions in smaller groups of two or three persons.

Pray Together

WORSHIP

Close the session, using this prayer or one of your own.

Pray together as a group. Share any prayer concerns you might have and write in the space below any prayer concerns shared by other persons.

O God, you have made us with different needs, thoughts, and wishes. Often that brings us into conflict with others. Teach us to solve conflicts in ways that are creative, just, and Christlike. Make us peacemakers in our families, our church, and our world. We bring our other concerns to you now, in Jesus' name. Amen.

(Pray aloud or silently for each of the prayer needs and concerns.)

CHAPTER FIVE

FAITH AND THE FAMILY

CHECKING-IN

Before group members start sharing, remind them to write down prayer concerns in the prayer section at the end of this session.

DISCUSSION POINT

BIBLE STUDY

DISCUSSION POINT

What are some important aspects you would include in a definition of faith?

Read and discuss the verses with your smaller group. Tell the larger group what the Bible verses say to you about faith.

What has been happening in your life in the past week about which you want the group to know?

What is coming up that you want the group to know about?

What happened with your family concerning the material covered in the last session or a previous session?

Faith and the Family

<u>What does it mean to be a Christian family? How does faith develop in children and adults? If parents have doubts about their faith, can children grow strong in faith?</u> Parents may have lots of questions about faith, but they may hesitate to voice them for a variety of reasons. Wondering about faith and discovering how persons grow in faith can enrich the faith of you and your children.

The Bible and Faith

As we discuss faith, it is important to see what the Bible means by faith. Divide the following Bible verses among smaller groups of two or three persons.

2 Timothy 1:5-7

Psalm 92:12-15

James 2:14-22

Hebrews 11:1-11

Hebrews 11:17-19

Hebrews 11:23-28

Hebrews 12:1-2

Colossians 2:6-7

DISCUSSION POINT

What do you think about this definition of faith?

What Is Faith?

Dictionaries define faith as loyalty to another person, being true to one's promises, systems of belief—including belief in God, and trust. For Christians to have faith in God means more than just to believe in God. It means to trust in God and to put your beliefs into actions. Religion is different from faith. Faith can be expressed through religion. Religion involves institutions, creeds, objects, and such. Religion has to do with knowing about the Bible. Christian faith involves living as a disciple of Jesus.

How Does Faith Happen?

We cannot teach our children faith or force them to have faith. They can learn what the Bible says or learn about church history or about our beliefs. But such knowledge does not automatically make them followers of Christ. As parents, we can find ways to help the faith of our children grow.

How does faith grow? John Westerhoff, author of *Will Our Children Have Faith?* (Seabury, 1976; page 89) suggests that, given proper experiences, faith expands through four styles. He has compared the growth in faith styles to growth of a tree. A small tree is a complete tree, even though it is smaller than a large tree. Similarly faith experienced in one style is still faith, even though it can expand and grow. Like a tree, faith needs proper nourishment to grow. A tree adds growth rings in an ever-expanding manner. Faith also grows in such a manner. Growth is added to what is already present. When you grow into the next style of faith, you still need the elements you needed in the earlier styles of faith.

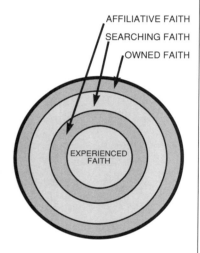

AFFILIATIVE FAITH
SEARCHING FAITH
OWNED FAITH
EXPERIENCED FAITH

Experienced Faith

During early childhood, children have what Westerhoff calls *experienced faith* (pages 91-93). They experience faith through actions and interactions. Children observe and explore, wonder and imagine, copy and create. They learn from the hugs they receive or don't receive. They learn whether people can be trusted to care for them or to ignore them. They begin to acquire language they later will need to understand and talk about their feelings, experiences, and new concepts. But experiences matter most.

The child connects words to experiences. To understand Christian concepts of love, trust, and acceptance, the child must have experiences of love, trust, and acceptance. Faith is experienced and expressed in interactions with others. Parents and other persons in the child's life need to share their faith through words and actions.

Affiliative Faith

After growing in *experienced faith* during childhood and early adolescence, persons may move on to a *faith of affiliation* (pages 94-96). This style of faith has three components: belonging to the religious community, experiencing religious feelings, and affirming the authority of the story and way of life of the faith community.

Persons in the affiliative style of faith need to belong to and feel they can make contributions to a community of faith. They need to participate in the activities with others. They need to feel accepted, wanted, and important to the faith community. Ways to belong may include joining the church, singing in the choir, ushering, serving on a committee, or collecting canned goods for the church food bank.

Religious feelings are important for affiliative faith. We need to experience awe and wonder, to feel the majesty of God. We need times to listen to and tell the Christian story in word, song, dance, art, and drama.

The third necessity for affiliative faith is learning the Christian story. Affiliative faith is not complete without this element. We must know the Christian faith story and heritage. We must hear and tell the story and act in such a way that it becomes our own story.

Searching Faith

The third style of faith (the one that seems most difficult for parents and churches to accept and deal with) is *searching faith* (pages 96-97). A person may begin to grow into this style of faith during late adolescence or early adulthood. However, this style may start even in mid-life or later, and some people may never grow into this style. In this style, the faith acquired earlier becomes subject to criticism and doubt. Westerhoff suggests that this style of faith also has three components.

1. *Doubt or critical judgment.* During this time serious study of

the Christian faith happens. Persons struggle with what the Christian story means. They hammer out theological, moral, and ethical understandings. They make critical judgments about their understandings.

2. *Experimentation.* Persons explore alternatives to their earlier faith and understandings. They test their own traditions by learning about other traditions. They discover more about their own faith by learning what it is not.

3. *Commitment.* Commitment enables us to give our lives to God, to persons, and to causes. Parents can find searching faith difficult because a searching person can seem so fickle, committing to one cause only to quickly give it up for another. Yet such experimentation helps us know what commitment is and learn how to commit ourselves to our faith.

Parents and congregations need to affirm that searching is a good and important style of faith. They need to support persons in their searching and doubting. Too often persons leave the church during this stage of faith. With no support in searching, they may stay in the searching and doubting style of faith for the rest of their lives. Finding ways to keep searchers within the community of faith during their intellectual struggles and their experimentation with alternate understandings is important.

GROUP INTERACTION

Divide the group into smaller groups no larger than four persons. Ask persons to share with their smaller group an issue of faith that they are currently facing. Then ask others in the group what ways they might suggest for dealing with that issue of faith.

Finding ways to help them with the needs of experienced faith and affiliative faith is also important, since searchers continue to have these needs during their searching and doubting.

Owned Faith

Only after searching and doubting can persons grow into *owned faith.* In this style of faith people are able to put their faith into action—their stated beliefs match their actions. Persons who commit themselves to the Christian faith try to follow God's will for their lives. They try to be Christlike in their actions. They fit the description in 1 John 2:6: "Whoever says, 'I abide in him,' ought to walk just as he walked." This style of faith happens only after needs of the other styles of faith have been met. This usually occurs after adolescence, perhaps in early adulthood or even much later. When persons move into this style of faith, they continue to need the experiences and interactions of experienced faith, the belonging and religious feelings of affiliative faith, and the continued seeking of searching faith.

GROUP INTERACTION

Divide the larger group into pairs. Ask persons to take turns within their pairs to share something that has been helpful to them as they have grown in faith.

The Role of the Congregation

A great variety of environments and experiences are necessary for faith to grow. Also needed are role models of persons who are in the expanded styles of faith. Some churches and congregations deal with some styles of faith better than with other styles of faith. Churches may inhibit or limit growth of faith by ignoring the needs of various faith styles. To encourage faith to grow, communities of faith need to meet the needs of persons in all the faith styles.

GROUP INTERACTION

Divide the group into four small groups. Assign one of the situations to each small group. Allow time for each group to discuss the situation, to choose roles, and to present the situation to the larger group.

Explore the Issues

Use what you have read about faith development to roleplay one or more of these situations:

Situation 1: Two or more parents of babies or young children meet with a pastor and a knowledgeable, experienced teacher of young children to ask about ways they can help their young children develop a strong Christian faith.

Situation 2: A late adolescent seriously questions some things in the Bible, such as how the Resurrection happened. The young person talks with a parent or other adult who knows that searching and doubting are an important stage of faith development.

Situation 3: Four adults meet as a committee to plan for the faith development of the elementary children of the church. Two adults know how faith grows. The other two adults want "a good strong program" but don't really know what that should be.

Situation 4: Three parents have a conversation about their personal needs to grow in faith. One parent is in the affiliative style of faith. One parent is in the searching style. The third parent is in the style of owned faith. As a result of their conversation, they decide to commend their church on what it is doing well and make some suggestions of ways to improve. Discuss these questions after each roleplay.

1. How did the roleplay characters show insight into faith development?

2. What questions or insights about developing faith popped into your mind during the roleplay?

3. What insights did you gain about what might be helpful in your own family? in your own congregation?

DISCUSSION POINT

Divide the larger group into two smaller groups. Assign each group one of these questions to discuss. After about ten minutes, invite both groups to report on their discussions.

Faith in a Wider Context

Using what you have learned about how faith grows, tell how you would address these concerns.

Some people say, "I don't need the church in order to be a Christian." How do you feel about this statement? What would you say to a person who expressed this idea?

Many children and adolescents are growing up with experiences that are very different from the ones needed for growth in Christian faith. What might Christians as individuals and as congregations do to address the faith needs of such persons?

Experiment and Practice

To act in faith, we must understand faith and decide how it relates to life. To put faith into action, we may use a cycle of action; reflection through study, prayer, and meditation; more action; and then more reflection.

With another group member, briefly practice using one of these models that can help you reflect on your faith in order to put your faith into action.

Model 1: Action/Reflection/Action

BIBLE STUDY & GROUP INTERACTION

For this activity you will need to have on hand these resources: Bible concordance; Bible dictionary; and Bible commentaries.

For practice, group members may suggest Bible verses or ways that the Christian faith might address an issue. Reflection on many issues can require much more time for in-depth study and thought.

1. Identify a parenting situation in which you took action today.

2. Reflect through Bible study, prayer, and meditation on how your Christian faith might have or could have addressed this situation. (You may need to study what the Bible has to say about principles involved in this issue. Use the resources listed in the marginal note as study materials.)

3. Plan a future action that reflects a way to put your faith into action in a similar situation.

Model 2: Reflection/Action

1. Identify a decision you need to make as a parent.

2. Inquire what the Christian faith has to say about it. Use Bible study, meditation, and prayer.

3. Make a plan that will incorporate your faith in your action.

Practice using one of the plans this week. On a level your child(ren) can understand, share what you are doing. If appropriate, use one of the plans as a family.

Measure the Group's Growth

Using the image of a tree, tell something about how you think the group is growing and why.

DISCUSSION POINT

Is the group leafing out or drying up? Is it still a sapling or is it becoming a more mature tree?

WORSHIP

Pray aloud or silently for each of the prayer needs and concerns.

Pray Together

As you pray to close this session, write the group's prayer concerns in the space below. To close, use the printed prayer or one in your own words.

O God, you have made us as persons who can grow in faith. As parents, we seek to know how to help our children grow in faith. In our life of faith together, we seek to support one another as we live in faith. We bring our concerns before you now, in Jesus' name. Amen.

CHAPTER SIX

LETTING GO

CHECKING-IN

What has been happening in your life in the past week that you want the group to know about?

What is coming up that you want the group to know about?

What happened with your family concerning the material covered in the last chapter or a previous chapter?

DISCUSSION POINT

Ask group members to share as many statements as they can think of that discourage independence, self-confidence, and self-reliance in a child. ("We don't have time for you to do it." "You always make a mess.")

Then share statements that encourage self-reliance, confidence, and independence in a child. ("You really used good judgment!" "You did it all by yourself!")

Letting Go Begins Early

Although "letting go" may seem an event that happens when a child leaves for college or gets married, the desire for independence develops early. The baby takes the spoon away from the person feeding him or her. The toddler insistently asserts, "Me do it!" Children are pleased with themselves when they have confidence to meet new challenges.

Experience is important in sharpening skills. A child learns to excel at a task by doing it over and over again. Parents encourage growing independence by allowing the child to try new tasks. Instead of claiming they are too young, we might find portions of a task with which the child can be successful.

Encourage Independence

Confidence and self-reliance take time, repeated efforts, ability for parents to tolerate mess and stress, and the ability to know when to provide support and when to refrain from interference. In a variety of ways, parents can thwart a child's efforts. A child may want to do a task, but the parent does not feel there is enough time. Or the parent does not want to deal with the mess. Or the parent may want to control the child's growing independence because the parent wants to be needed. When we discourage a child's efforts to develop self-reliance and independence, we lose the opportunity to teach important skills, to let the child learn from doing, and we prevent the child from strengthening self-esteem. When we encourage the child to try new skills and to practice them, we encourage the child to learn how to be independent.

Feeling successful is an important part of moving toward self-confidence and self-reliance. Children feel successful and confident when parents recognize and praise their efforts and accomplishments. Parents can refrain from criticizing less-than-perfect results when children are excited about doing a task. Parents might refrain from showing a better way until later when the thrill of accomplishment won't be damaged. To help a child grow in independence and self-reliance, it is helpful to stick with positive comments about the child's efforts and accomplishments. Negative criticism destroys self-esteem and motivation.

Readiness is important for success in developing independence. Is the child ready to do what he or she wants to try? Is the child ready for what the parent is insisting that the child do? Some children are not ready for certain kinds of independence, even when children think they are or when their parents wish they would be ready. Children are harmed when parents expect maturity beyond their abilities. Unrealistic expectations damage self-esteem and confidence. Other consequences can be dangerous and even deadly. On the other hand, underestimating a child's abilities and expecting too little can also reduce a child's self-confidence and make the child unwilling to do things for himself or herself. Delaying appropriate opportunities for independence can reduce a child's capabilities and make the child further dependent or rebellious.

WRITTEN REFLECTION

Think of one way your child is trying to or needs to become self-reliant. Record your thoughts below:

WRITTEN REFLECTION

Think of a way you can help your child to develop skills needed for confidence and self-reliance. ("My child is going away on a trip. I need to help him learn how to make a collect call.") Record your thoughts below:

Determine Readiness

To judge readiness, compare the child to groups of children of the same age or same stage of development. Be aware of child development and sequences in which children develop capabilities. Watch for the child's interest in learning how to do a new task. However, interest alone is not a definite indicator of readiness. Some children beg to drive from the time they can talk!

A parent should provide support when needed as a child moves toward self-reliance and independence. Besides allowing the child to try new experiences, a parent can teach needed skills or arrange for the child to learn them, provide encouragement, and let the child know that it is okay to make mistakes. Even when a parent cannot be physically present, the parent can be emotionally available to the child. ("You can call me anytime—even when I am in a meeting.")

Letting go means coming to terms with both the strengths and limitations of the particular child, regardless of the child's age. We know that letting go can involve consequences—in some instances consequences of great magnitude. We may want to protect the child, solve his or her problems, be in control, and feel needed.

Decide if Letting Go Is Helpful or Harmful

Letting go can be helpful or harmful to a child. Helpful letting go takes place in relation to the child's need. Harmful letting go takes place when the parent's needs are placed above the child's needs. Children can be harmed physically and emotionally when they are expected to be independent and self-reliant before they have the skills or when given inadequate support. When a parent gives up appropriate responsibility and forces the child into too much self-reliance, the child becomes a victim of neglect.

DISCUSSION POINT

What feelings do you have about letting go of your child?

When was a time that was difficult?

What helped you and your child?

Ask group members to share ideas, methods of coping, or resources they have found helpful in letting go. Record them on chalkboard or newsprint, if available.

DISCUSSION POINT

Turn Over Responsibility

Sometimes parents need to step back and allow the child to take responsibility. <u>For example, whose responsibility is it to make sure your child has his or her school books to do that night's assignment? Should you make a frantic trip back to the school before it closes? Or should you let the child take the consequences of not having completed the assignment?</u>

Natural or logical consequences can be a good partner. Instead of trying to control the child, the parent can make the child responsible for certain problems. When a parent steps back and makes the child responsible for decisions and mistakes, the child can feel pride in making good decisions and the child can learn from mistakes, especially when mistakes are seen as a natural part of learning.

DISCUSSION POINT

What might you say to your child to help him or her understand that mistakes are okay?

Children are more willing to try new tasks and experiences when parents make it clear that it is acceptable to make mistakes. Parents can say in words and show by their actions that mistakes are to be expected when persons try things that are new. Children should understand that they are not loved any less if they make mistakes.

Trusting a child to be capable and allowing the child the opportunity to make mistakes and learn from them is both respectful and caring. It gives the child confidence and prevents the child from being crippled by a parent who is willing to do too much.

DISCUSSION POINT

What kind of feelings can you anticipate having as you let go?

Recognize Ambivalent Feelings

Letting go usually involves a mix of feelings. A child's growing self-reliance may represent ends to certain stages in a parent's life as well as the child's. A parent may see growing independence as loss of control over children and their lives, a realization that the parent is no longer needed in quite the same way as before, a message that the parent is left out, left behind, and getting old. On the other hand, a parent can find it exciting to watch children face challenges and tackle them successfully.

GROUP INTERACTION

In smaller groups, develop a simulated roleplay in which parents and children talk about their mixed feelings over letting go. Allow time for each smaller group to present its roleplay to the larger group.

BIBLE STUDY

DISCUSSION POINT

What other Bible stories and passages can you think of that show us that God gave human beings the freedom to choose?

In what ways might we learn from the consequences of wise and unwise choices?

BIBLE STUDY

Divide the stories among smaller groups. Ask the smaller groups first to discuss what the stories say about parents letting go of children, and then have them share their discoveries with the larger group.

For the child, letting go is a significant experience. It can be both exciting and frightening. The child may venture forth bravely one day and seek to remain protected and cared for another. A child or teen can be confused by his or her own feelings as well as by the parent's feelings. Parents may alternate between coaxing the child to be independent and wanting the child to stay dependent just a little while longer. Messages to children are often mixed. We may want our children to make their own decisions, but we want them to decide to do what we think is best. We may want children to use their judgment, but we want them to follow our advice. It is helpful to both the child and the parent when the parent can recognize ambivalent feelings. Then the parent can send fewer mixed messages. Sometimes children and parents find it helpful to talk with one another about their mixed feelings.

God Also Lets Go

God knows a lot about letting go. God created human beings as persons who could choose what they would do, not robots who would automatically do what was best. God instructed Moses to tell the Hebrew people, "If you obey my voice and keep my covenant, you shall be my treasured possession . . ." (Exodus 19:5). Jesus recognized that persons are free to make choices about their actions. In John 13:17, Jesus says, "If you know these things, you are blessed if you do them." Jesus knew that human behavior always involves "if you do." Throughout the Old and New Testament, the Bible stresses the rewards of certain choices and the consequences of other choices. God made us free and allows us freedom to make certain choices. God lets us know the consequences of wise and unwise actions. Then God trusts us to make a choice and learn from it.

Letting go is part of our growth as parents. When children are well-prepared for independence and self-reliance, parents can let go more easily and realize that they have done their job well.

Some Bible Parents Who Let Go

In the Bible we find some stories of parents who let their children go. Read one or more of these stories:

Genesis 16:1-4,15; 21:1-3, 8-20—Abraham and his son Ishmael. (God changed Abram's and Sarai's names to Abraham and Sarah. Ishmael was fourteen years older than Isaac.)

Exodus 1:22; 2:1-10—Moses and his mother.

1 Samuel 1:1-28; 2:11, 18-19—Hannah and her son Samuel.

Luke 2:41-52—Mary and Joseph and twelve-year-old Jesus.

Luke 15:11-22—the loving father and the prodigal son.

DISCUSSION POINT

Remembering that Bible people lived in a different time and culture, think about some ways that letting go may have been positive and/or negative. <u>Do you see any similarities to what is happening today? What lessons do you find in these stories that could help you with your own process of letting go?</u>

GROUP INTERACTION

Ask smaller groups to look at one or more of the situations. Ask them to tell what issues each situation involves. Discuss how much letting go might be done or should be done. Smaller groups might roleplay a positive way and a negative way to let go in one or more of the situations.

Explore the Issues

Use these situations to explore the issues of letting go:

1. Michiko, a fourth grader, wants to learn to play the saxophone. Her mother thinks that the violin is a better instrument.

2. Benjamin is eleven. His brothers and sister are 8, 6, and 5. Benjamin knows the family needs money and wants to help out by babysitting the other children all day during the summer while his mother works.

3. Kyla is a freshman in college. She is having difficulties with her roommate about the roommate's loud, constant music. Her father insists that she switch roommates.

4. Jason is four. He likes to dress himself. He chooses clothes that are appropriate for the weather, but his family doesn't like some of the combinations he wants to wear to preschool.

Letting Go in a Wider Context

American society as a whole is "letting go" of children more and more without providing proper supports. Very young children are being left alone with no supervision because childcare is expensive and may be unavailable. Teenage pregnancy and births to unwed mothers are higher than ever before. A high percentage of teens drop out before high school graduation. Suicides among adolescents and even among young children are increasing. Alcohol and drug abuse are appearing among ever-younger elementary school children.

Some or all these cases may be "somebody else's children." Yet these situations touch all our lives. If they are not your own children, they may be the children next door or down the block, children at school with your children, or children in another town and state. But what happens to these children affects us and our children. Extra taxes, crime, disrupted classrooms where learning cannot take place, or unwholesome influences on our children are only some of the results.

DISCUSSION POINT

How does your church address situations such as latchkey children, children at risk of dropping out of school, children and teens involved in alcohol and drug abuse? What else can it do? What supports does your denomination provide for unwed mothers, for crack babies, or babies and parents with AIDS? You are only one person, but how might you make a positive difference in what is happening to today's children?

Letting Go of the Group

CHECKING IN

Give group members the option of sharing or not sharing their reflections.

Think back over the weeks that the group has been together. How effective has the group been in preparing you and other group members for greater self-confidence in parenting? As your study ends, how do you feel about letting go of the group? (Write your reflections below.)

DISCUSSION POINT

Some groups may choose to continue to meet together, either over parenting concerns or to begin another LIFESEARCH study.

How do you plan to let go of one another? How might you still provide one another support and encouragement as you let go?

Pray Together

WORSHIP

As you close this session, take several moments to worship together. Share prayer concerns and joys.

Some groups may choose to end this LIFESEARCH study by inviting a pastor to celebrate Holy Communion with them.

Use this prayer or one of your own.

O God, you have given us children to hold, love, guide and nurture. As parents, we seek to know how and when to let our children go. We seek your support, guidance, and wisdom as we experience the pains and the joys of seeing our children grow in confidence and self-reliance toward independence. We bring these concerns before you now, in Jesus' name. Amen.

(Pray aloud or silently for each of the prayer needs and concerns.)

THE LIFESEARCH GROUP EXPERIENCE

Every LIFESEARCH group will be different. Because your group is made up of unique individuals, your group's experience will also be unique. No other LIFESEARCH group will duplicate the dynamics, feelings, and adventures your group will encounter.

And yet as we planned LIFESEARCH, we had a certain vision in mind about what we hoped might happen as people came together to use a LIFESEARCH book for discussion and support around a common concern. Each LIFESEARCH book focuses on some life concern of adults within a Christian context over a six-session course. LIFESEARCH books have been designed to be easy to lead, to encourage group nurture, and to be biblically based and needs-oriented.

Each chapter in this LIFESEARCH book has been designed for use during a one and one-half hour group session. In each LIFESEARCH book, you will find
• times for group members to "check in" with each other concerning what has gone on in their lives during the past week and what they wish to share from the past week concerning the material covered in the group sessions;
• times for group members to "check in" about how they are doing as a group;
• substantial information/reflection/discussion segments, often utilizing methods such as case studies and simulation;
• Bible study segments;
• segments in which a specific skill or process is introduced, tried out, and/or suggested for use during the week to come;
• segments that help group participants practice supporting one another with the concerns being explored.

LIFESEARCH was not planned with the usual one hour Sunday school class in mind. If you intend to use LIFESEARCH with a Sunday school class, you will need to adapt it to the length of time you have available. Either plan to take more than one week to discuss each chapter or be less ambitious with what you aim to accomplish in a session's time.

LIFESEARCH was also not planned to be used in a therapy group, a sensitivity group, or an encounter group.

No one is expected to be an expert on the topic. No one is expected to offer psychological insights into what is going on. However, we do hope that LIFESEARCH group members will offer one another support and Christian love.

We will count LIFESEARCH as successful if you find your way to thought-provoking discussions centered around information, insights, and helps providing aid for living everyday life as Christians.

You might find it helpful to see what we envisioned a sample LIFESEARCH group might experience. Keep in mind, however, that your experience might be quite different. Leave room for your creativity and uniqueness. Remain receptive to God's Spirit.

> A LIFESEARCH group is simply a group of persons who come together to struggle together from a Christian perspective with a common life concern.

You sit in the living room of a friend from church for the second session of your LIFESEARCH group. Besides you and your host, four other persons are present, sitting on the sofa and overstuffed chairs. You, your host, your group leader, and one other are church members, although not all of you make it to church that regularly. The remaining two persons are neighbors of the leader. You chat while a light refreshment and beverage are served by the host.

Your leader offers a brief prayer, and then asks each of you to share what has been going on in your lives during the past week since you last met. One member shares about a spouse who had outpatient surgery. Several mention how hectic the week was with the usual work- and family-related demands. Prayer concerns and requests are noted.

This session begins with a written reflection. The leader draws your attention to a brief question in the beginning of the chapter you were assigned to read for today. Group members are asked to think about the question and write a short response.

While the leader records responses on a small chalkboard brought for that purpose, members take turns sharing something from their written reflections. A brief discussion follows when one group member mentions something she had never noticed before.

Group members respond as the leader asks for any reports concerning trying out the new life skill learned in the previous session. Chuckles, words of encouragement, and suggestions for developing the new skill further pepper the reports.

The leader notes one of the statements made in the assigned chapter from the LIFESEARCH book and asks to what extent the statement is true to the experience of the group members. Not much discussion happens on this point, since everyone agrees the statement is true. But one of the members presses on to the next statement in the LIFESEARCH book, and all sorts of conversation erupts! All six group members have their hot buttons pushed.

Your leader calls the group to move on to Bible study time. You read over the text, and then participate in a dramatic reading in which everyone has a part. During the discussion that follows the reading, you share some insights that strike you for the first time because you identify with the person whose role you read.

You and the other group members take turns simulating a simple technique suggested in the book for dealing with a specific concern. Everyone coaches everyone else; and what could have been an anxiety-producing experience had you remained so self-conscious, quickly becomes both fun and helpful. You and one of the other group members agree to phone each other during the week to find out how you're doing with practicing this technique in real life.

It's a few minutes later than the agreed upon time to end, but no one seems to mind. You read together a prayer printed at the end of this week's chapter.

On the way out to your car, you ponder how quickly the evening has passed. You feel good about what you've learned and about deepening some new friendships. You look forward to the next time your LIFESEARCH group meets.

This has been only one model of how a LIFESEARCH group session might turn out. Yours will be different. But as you give it a chance, you will learn some things and you will

STARTING A
LifeSearch GROUP

The key ingredient to starting a LifeSearch group is *interest*. People are more likely to get excited about those things in which they are interested. People are more likely to join a group to study and to work on those areas of their lives in which they are interested.

Interest often comes when there is some itch to be scratched in a person's life, some anxiety to be soothed, or some pain to be healed.

Are persons interested in the topic of a LifeSearch book? Or, perhaps more important to ask, do they have needs in their lives that can be addressed using a LifeSearch book?

If you already have an existing group that finds interesting one of the topics covered by the LifeSearch books, go for it! Just keep in mind that LifeSearch is intended more as a small-group resource than as a class study textbook.

If you want to start a new group around LifeSearch, you can begin in one of two ways:

- You can begin with a group of interested people and let them choose from among the topics LifeSearch offers; or

- You can begin with one of the LifeSearch topics and locate people who are interested in forming a group around that topic.

What is the right size for a LifeSearch group? Well, how many persons do you have who are interested?

Actually, LifeSearch is intended as a *small-group* resource. The best size is between four and eight persons. Under four persons will make it difficult to carry out some of the group interactions. Over eight and not everyone will have a good opportunity to participate. The larger the group means the less time each person has to share.

If you have more than eight persons interested in your LifeSearch group, why not start two groups?

Or if you have a group larger than eight that just does not want to split up, then be sure to divide into smaller groups of no more than eight for discussion times. LifeSearch needs the kind of interaction and discussion that only happen in small groups.

How do you find out who is interested in LifeSearch? One good way is for you to sit down with a sheet of paper and list the names of persons whom you think might be interested. Even better would be for you to get one or two other people to brainstorm names with you. Then start asking. Call them on the telephone. Or visit them

> **Interest often comes when there is some itch to be scratched in a person's life, some anxiety to be soothed, or some pain to be healed.**

in person. People respond more readily to personal invitations.

When you invite persons and they seem interested in LIFESEARCH, ask them if they will commit to attending all six sessions. Emergencies do arise, of course. However, the group's life is enhanced if all members participate in all sessions.

LIFESEARCH is as much a group experience as it is a time for personal learning.

As you plan to begin a LIFESEARCH group, you will need to answer these questions:

- **Who will lead the group?** Will you be the leader for all sessions? Do you plan to rotate leadership among the group members? Do you need to recruit an individual to serve as group leader?

- **Where will you meet?** You don't have to meet at a church. In fact, if you are wanting to involve a number of persons not related to your church, a neutral site might be more appropriate. Why not hold your meetings at a home? But if you

do, make sure plans are made to hold distractions and interruptions to a minimum. Send the children elsewhere and put the answering machine on. Keep any refreshments simple.

- **How will you get the LIFESEARCH books to group members before the first session?** You want to encourage members to read the first chapter in advance of the first session. Do you need to have an initial gathering some days before the first discussion sessions in order to hand out books and take care of other housekeeping matters? Do you need to mail or otherwise transport the books to group members?

Most LIFESEARCH groups will last only long enough to work through the one LIFESEARCH book in which there is interest. Be open, however, to the possibility of either continuing your LIFESEARCH group as a support group around the life issue you studied, or as a group to study another topic in the LIFESEARCH series.

TIPS FOR LIVELY DISCUSSIONS

TIP 1

Don't lecture. You are responsible for leading a discussion, not for conveying information.

TIP 4

Recognize when the silence has gone on long enough. Some questions do fall flat. Some questions exhaust themselves. Some silence means that people really have nothing more to say. You'll come to recognize different types of silences with experience.

TIP 2

Ask open-ended questions. Ask: How would you describe the color of the sky? Don't ask: Is the sky blue?

TIP 5

If Plan A doesn't work to stimulate lively discussion, move on to Plan B. Each chapter in this LIFESEARCH book contains more discussion starters and group interaction ideas than you can use in an hour and a half. If something doesn't work, move on and try something else.

TIP 3

Allow silence. Sometimes, some people need to think about something before they say anything. The WRITTEN REFLECTIONS encourage this kind of thought.

TIP 6

Let the group lead you in leading discussion. Let the group set the agenda. If you lead the group in the direction you want to go, you might discover that no one is following you. You are leading to serve the group, not to serve yourself.

Ask follow-up questions. If some-one makes a statement or offers a response, ask: Why do you say that? Better yet, ask a different group member: What do you think of so-and-so's statement?

Do your own homework. Read the assigned chapter. Plan out possible directions for the group session to go based on the leader's helps in the text. Plan options in case your first plan doesn't work out. Know the chapter's material.

Know your group. Think about the peculiar interests and needs of the specific individuals within your group. Let your knowledge of the group shape the direction in which you lead the discussion.

Don't try to accomplish everything. Each chapter in this LifeSearch book offers more leader's helps in the form of DISCUSSION POINTS, GROUP INTERACTIONS, and other items than you can use in one session. So don't try to use them all! People become frustrated with group discussions that try to cover too much ground.

Don't let any one person dominate the discussion—including yourself. (See "Dealing with Group Prob-lems," page 58.")

Encourage, but don't force, persons who hold back from participation. (See "Dealing with Group Prob-lems," page 58.)

TAKING YOUR GROUP'S TEMPERATURE

How do you tell if your LIFESEARCH group is healthy? If it were one human being, you could take its temperature with a thermometer and discover whether body temperature seemed to be within a normal range. Taking the temperature of a group is more complex and less precise. But you can try some things to get a sense of how healthily your group is progressing.

✔ **Find out whether the group is measuring up to what the members expected of it.** During the CHECKING IN portion of the first session, you are asked to record what members say as they share why they came to this LIFESEARCH group. At a later time you can bring out that sheet and ask how well the LIFESEARCH experience measures up to satisfying why people came in the first place.

✔ **Ask how members perceive the group dynamics.** Say: On a scale from one as the lowest to ten as the highest, where would you rate the overall participation by members of this group? On the same scale where would you rate this LIFESEARCH group as meeting your needs? On the same scale where would you rate the "togetherness" of this LIFESEARCH group?

You can make up other appropriate questions to help you get a sense of the temperature of the group.

✔ **Ask group members to fill out an evaluation sheet on the LIFESEARCH experience.** Keep the evaluation form simple.

One of the simplest forms leaves plenty of blank space for responding to three requests: (1) Name the three things you would want to do more of. (2) Name the three things you would want to do less of. (3) Name the three things you would keep about the same.

✔ **Debrief a LIFESEARCH session with one of the other participants.** Arrange ahead of time for a group member to stay a few minutes after a meeting or to meet with you the next day. Ask for direct feedback about what seemed to work or not work, who seems to be participating well, who seems to be dealing with something particularly troubling, and so forth.

✔ **Give group members permission to say when they sense something is not working.** As the group leader, you do not hold responsibility for the life of the group. The group's life belongs to *all* the members of the group. Encourage group members to take responsibility for what takes place within the group session.

✔ **Expect and accept that, at times, discussion starters will fall flat, group interaction will seem stilted, group members will be grumpy.** All groups have bad days. Moreover all groups go through their own life cycles. Although six sessions may not be enough time for your LIFESEARCH group to gel completely, you may find that after two or three sessions, one session will come when nothing seems to go right. That is normal. In fact, studies show that only those groups that first show a little conflict ever begin to move into deeper levels of relationship.

✔ **Sit back and observe.** In the middle of a DISCUSSION POINT or GROUP INTER-ACTION, sit back and try to look at the group as a whole. Does it look healthy to you? Is one person dominating? Does someone else seem to be withdrawn? How would you describe what you observe going on within the group at that time?

✔ **Take the temperature of the group—really!** No, not with a thermometer. But try asking the group to take its own temperature. Would it be normal? below normal? feverish? What adjective would you use to describe the group's temperature?

✔ **Keep a temperature record.** At least keep some notes from session to session on how you think the health of the group looks to you. Then after later sessions, you can look back on your notes from earlier sessions and see how your group has changed.

LifeSearch Group Temperature Record

Chapter 1
_____
_____
_____

Chapter 4
_____
_____
_____

Chapter 2
_____
_____
_____

Chapter 5
_____
_____
_____

Chapter 3
_____
_____
_____

Chapter 6
_____
_____
_____

DEALING WITH GROUP PROBLEMS

What do you do if your group just does not seem to be working out?

First, figure out what is going on. The ideas in "Taking Your Group's Temperature" (pages 56-57) will help you to do this. If you make the effort to observe and listen to your group, you should be able to anticipate and head off many potential problems.

Second, remember that the average LIFE-SEARCH group will only be together for six weeks—the average time needed to study one LIFESEARCH book. Most new groups will not have the chance to gel much in such a short period of time. Don't expect the kind of group development and nurture you might look for in a group that has lived and shared together for years.

Third, keep in mind that even though you are a leader, the main responsibility for how the group develops belongs to the group itself. You do the best you can to create a hospitable setting for your group's interactions. You do your homework to keep the discussion and interactions flowing. But ultimately, every member of the group individually and corporately bear responsibility for whatever happens within the life of the group.

However, if these specific problems do show up, try these suggestions:

✓ One Member Dominates the Group

• Help the group to identify this problem for itself by asking group members to state on a scale from one as the lowest to ten as the highest where they would rank overall participation within the group.

• Ask each member to respond briefly to a DISCUSSION POINT in a round robin fashion. It may be helpful to ask the member who dominates to respond toward the end of the round robin.

• Practice gate-keeping by saying, "We've heard from Joe; now what does someone else think?"

• If the problem becomes particularly troublesome, speak gently outside of a group session with the member who dominates.

✓ One Member Is Reluctant to Participate

• Ask each member to respond briefly to a DISCUSSION POINT in a round robin fashion.

• Practice gate-keeping for reluctant participants by saying, "Sam, what would you say about this?"

• Increase participation by dividing the larger group into smaller groups of two or three persons.

✓ The Group Chases Rabbits Instead of Staying With the Topic

• Judge whether the rabbit is really a legitimate or significant concern for the group to be discussing. By straying from your agenda, is the group setting an agenda more valid for their needs?

• Restate the original topic or question.

• Ask why the group seems to want to avoid a particular topic or question.

• If one individual keeps causing the group to stray inappropriately from the topic, speak with him or her outside of a session.

✔ Someone Drops Out of the Group

• A person might drop out of the group because his or her needs are not being met within the group. You will never know this unless you ask that person directly.

• Contact a person immediately following the first absence. Otherwise they are unlikely to return.

✔ The Group or Some of Its Members Remain on a Superficial Level of Discussion

• In a six-session study, you cannot necessarily expect enough trust to develop for a group to move deeper than a superficial level.

• Never press an individual member of a LIFESEARCH group to disclose anything more than they are comfortable doing so in the group.

• Encourage an atmosphere of confidentiality within the group. Whatever is said within the group, stays within the group.

✔ Someone Shares a Big, Dangerous, or Bizarre Problem

• LIFESEARCH groups are not therapy groups. You should not take on the responsibility of "fixing" someone else's problem.

• Encourage a member who shares a major problem to seek professional help.

• If necessary, remind the group about the need for confidentiality.

• If someone shares something that endangers either someone else or himself/herself, contact your pastor or a professional caregiver (psychologist, social worker, physician, attorney) for advice.

IF YOU'RE NOT LEADING THE GROUP

> **Be sure to read this article if you are *not* the person with specific responsibility for leading your LIFESEARCH group.**

If you want to get the most out of your LIFESEARCH group and this LIFESEARCH book, try the following suggestions.

✔ **Make a commitment to attend all the group sessions and participate fully.** An important part of the LIFESEARCH experience takes place within your group. If you miss a session, you miss out on the group life. Also, your group will miss what you would have added.

✔ **Read the assigned chapter in your LIFESEARCH book ahead of time.** If you are familiar with what the MAIN TEXT of the LIFESEARCH book says, you will be able to participate more fully in discussions and group interactions.

✔ **Try the activities suggested in BEFORE NEXT TIME.** Contributions you make to the group discussion based upon your experiences will enrich the whole group. Moreover, LIFESEARCH will only make a real difference in your life if you try out new skills and behaviors outside of the group sessions.

✔ **Keep confidences shared within the group.** Whatever anyone says within the group needs to stay within the group. Help make your group a safe place for persons to share their deeper thoughts, feelings, and needs.

✔ **Don't be a "problem" participant.** Certain behaviors will tend to cause difficulties within the life of any group. Read the article on "Dealing with Group Problems," on pages 58-59. Do any of these problem situations describe you? Take responsibility for your own group behavior, and change your behavior as necessary for the sake of the health of the whole group.

✔ **Take your turn as a group leader, if necessary.** Some LIFESEARCH groups will rotate group leadership among their members. If this is so for your LIFESEARCH group, accept your turn gladly. Read the other leadership articles in the back of this LIFESEARCH book. Relax, do your best, and have fun leading your group.

✔ **Realize that all group members exercise leadership within a group.** The health of your group's life belongs to all the group members, not just to the leader alone. What can you do to help your group become healthier and more helpful to its members? Be a "gatekeeper" for persons you notice are not talking much. Share a thought or a feeling if the discussion is slow to start. Back off from sharing your perspective if you sense you are dominating the discussion.

✔ **Take responsibility for yourself.** Share concerns, reflections, and opinions related to the topic at hand as appropriate. But keep in mind that the group does not exist to "fix" your problems. Neither can you "fix" anyone else's problems, though from time to time it may be appropriate to share insights on what someone else is facing based upon your own experience and wisdom. Instead of saying, "What you need to do is . . ." try saying, "When I have faced a similar situation, I have found it helpful to . . ."

✔ **Own your own statements.** Instead of saying, "Everyone knows such and so is true," try saying "I believe such and so is true, because . . . ." Or instead of saying "That will never work," try saying, "I find it hard to see how that will work. Can anyone help me see how it might work?" Instead of saying, "That's dumb!" try saying, "I have a hard time accepting that statement because . . . ."

OUR LifeSearch GROUP

Name	Address	Phone Number

FEEDBACK MAIL-IN SHEET

✂ CUT HERE

Please tell us what you liked and disliked about LIFESEARCH:

4. The two things I like best about this LIFESEARCH experience were

5. The two things I liked least about this LIFESEARCH experience were

6. The two things I would have done differently if I had designed this LIFESEARCH book are

7. Topics for which you should develop new LIFESEARCH books are

8. I want to be sure to say the following about LIFESEARCH.

9. I led _____ sessions of this LIFESEARCH book.

FOLD HERE

Thank you for taking the time to fill out and return this feedback questionnaire.

Please check the LIFESEARCH book you are evaluating.

☐ Spiritual Gifts ☐ Health and Wholeness
☐ Juggling Demands ☐ Stress
☐ Parenting ☐ The Environment

Please tell us about your group:

1. Our group had an average attendance of _____.

2. Our group was made up of
   _____ young adults (19 through 25 years of age).
   _____ adults mostly between 25 and 45 years of age.
   _____ adults mostly between 45 and 60 years of age.
   _____ adults 60 and over.
   _____ a mixture of ages.

3. Our group (answer as many as apply)
   _____ came together for the sole purpose of studying this LIFESEARCH book.
   _____ has decided to study another LIFESEARCH book.
   _____ is an ongoing Sunday school class.
   _____ met at a time other than Sunday morning.
   _____ had only one leader for this LIFESEARCH study.

Name_____

Address_____

_____

Telephone_____

Editor, LIFESEARCH series
Church School Publications
P. O. Box 801
Nashville, Tennessee 37202

STAPLE OR TAPE HERE